A LIFE That MATTERS

Spiritual Disciplines That Change the World

JOANNE STUART SLOAN
CHERYL SLOAN WRAY

New Hope Publishers
Birmingham, Alabama

New Hope Publishers
P. O. Box 12065
Birmingham, AL 35283-0010
www.newhopepubl.com

Library of Congress Cataloging-in-Publication Data
Sloan, C. Joanne (Cheryl Joanne), 1947-
A life that matters : spiritual disciplines that change the world /
Joanne Stuart Sloan, Cheryl Sloan Wray.
p. cm.
ISBN 1-56309-719-2 (softcover)
1. Christian women—Religious life. 2. Spiritual life—Christianity.
I. Wray, Cheryl Sloan. II. Title.
BV4527 .S53 2002
248.8'43—dc21
2001007173

Cover design by Janell E. Young

ISBN: 1-56309-719-2
N024114•0302•5M1

To Virginia Stuart and Fay Sloan—

Your lives of faith inspired us to seek and serve God.

"I have been reminded of your sincere faith, which first lived in your grandmother Lois and in your mother Eunice and, I am persuaded, now lives in you also" (2 Tim. 1:5).

Contents

Acknowledgements

Many individuals helped make this book possible. They were kind enough to let us use their stories, gave us much needed encouragement and inspiration, and prayed fervently for us!

We thank, first of all, the men and women who shared with us the stories of their own Christian walk. Their interviews were invaluable as we composed chapters on the various spiritual disciplines.

We must acknowledge the amazing legacy of historical Christians. Their understanding of and practice of the various spiritual disciplines demonstrate to us what it means to follow Christ.

We want to thank our editor, Jan Turrentine, who encouraged us throughout the process. We are indebted to a fellow writer, Sammie Barstow, whose interest and help we so appreciate.

Thanks also to the many family members and friends who encouraged us. Without their inspiration and constant prayers, we would not have been able to complete this book.

To Christopher and Danielle, our son and brother and daughter-in-law and sister-in-law, we thank them for their interest and encouragement. To our dear husbands, David and Gary, we are eternally grateful. To David who provided us with wonderful insights and to Gary who kept telling us we could do it, we cannot thank them enough.

To the many readers who will read this book, we pray that it will inspire and motivate you to make these spiritual disciplines a priority in your lives.

JOANNE STUART SLOAN
CHERYL SLOAN WRAY

Introduction

"Let all our employment be to know God; the more one knows him, the more one desires to know him."—Brother Lawrence in *The Practice of the Presence of God*

How can we better know God? How can we have an intimate relationship with Him?

The answer comes in the form of spiritual disciplines. By making spiritual practices an integral part of our lives, we will draw closer to God and, in turn, we can have a greater impact on the the world.

A Life That Matters: Spiritual Disciplines That Change the World introduces (or reintroduces) you to these spiritual disciplines. Using the book as a guide, you can incorporate these disciplines into your daily life.

Pastor and author Charles Stanley says that all Christians have a basic understanding of why discipline is important, even if they don't practice it.

"Down through the ages, Christians have known that when they practice basic spiritual disciplines—reading God's word daily, praying often, giving faithfully, attending church regularly, staying active in outreach ministries—they are much more likely to hear from God, experience God's love, joy, and peace, grow in the effective use of their talents, receive blessings beyond anything they had asked or imagined."

He adds, "We never grow beyond our need for the basics. They are the foundation on which all other aspects of our Christian life are built. They are the disciplines that need to become deeply ingrained habits in us."

Just as we nourish our physical bodies, we must nourish our inner lives. The Bible teaches that what a person is inside is more important than his or her outward appearance or economic or social status. "For the Lord does not see as man sees; for man looks at the outward appearance, but the Lord looks at the heart" (1 Sam. 16:7).

Christ had strong words for the Pharisees who neglected their inner life but gave extra attention to their outward expressions of religion. In Matthew 23:25–26, He said, "You clean the outside of the cup and dish, but inside they are full of greed and indulgence. You blind Pharisees! First clean the inside of the cup and dish, and then the outside will also be clean."

Today, people spend hours in gyms developing their physical bodies. Our bodies are temples of God, and we should keep them in good shape so we can be of service to God. However, we often neglect our inner life. As the Apostle Paul said, "Train yourself to be godly. For physical training is of some value, but godliness has value for all things, holding promise for both the present life and the life to come" (1 Tim. 4:7–8).

The late great Baptist scholar Herschel H. Hobbs rightly said, "A person is not a body nor does he or she have a soul. A person is a soul that indwells a body, and one whose primary need is spiritual fitness."

Author and women's leader Esther Burroughs says that spiritual disciplines are essential if we are to grow as Christians. "In my opinion, there is no other way to follow Christ than to have a disciplined walk with him. And discipline has a purpose," Esther says. "In Hebrews, we read, 'For our earthly fathers disciplined us for only a short period of time and chastised us as seemed proper and good for them; but He disciplines us for our certain good, that we may become sharers in His own holiness.'"

Richard J. Foster, whose classic book *The Celebration of Discipline* reinvigorated interest in the disciplined life, said, "We should be willing to study and explore the spiritual life with all the rigor and determination we would give to any field of research."

Wife, mother, and author Kathy Collard Miller says that it's imperative to find time and energy to practice the disciplines. "Without taking the time and effort to practice the spiritual disciplines, we literally cannot know God intimately. It's through things like Bible study, prayer, meditation, and worship that we learn who God is, what He desires for us, and how to be empowered by His Spirit," she says. "The spiritual disciplines are the foundation for our faith and if it's crumbling, we're not going to be able to stand strong, especially in a moment of temptation."

This book attempts to discuss the spiritual disciplines in a fresh way. We have chosen to examine 12 spiritual disciplines: prayer, Bible study, worship, personal witnessing, solitude, journaling, personal study, guidance, simplicity, stewardship, service, and sacrifice. Within these 12 chapters we have also included the disciplines of meditation, fasting, confession, fellowship, and obedience. This is by no means an exhaustive list of spiritual disciplines, but it is a collection of the disciplines we deem most necessary in our lives today.

This book presents information about these disciplines through explanation and illustrations. These illustrations come from people—both historical and contemporary—who exemplify what a life that matters is all about. They have practiced, and still practice today, the different disciplines in a way that has drawn them closer to God.

Spiritual habits of devotion toward God have been practiced since biblical times, and countless Christians throughout the ages have modeled lives committed to the Lord. They found that to be of service to God and to others they had to nurture their inner lives. Their experiences and insights have come down to us in great classic works such as devotionals, autobiographies, biographies, sermons, poetry, drama, and novels. We have attempted to share as many of their stories as possible in this book.

Christians today—writers, nurses, secretaries, ministers, homemakers, business persons, and countless more—incorporate spiritual disciplines daily into their lives. Their stories will inspire you to make the disciplines a more meaningful part of your life.

Practicing these disciplines just to practice them, however, is not the point. We must be doing them with the right attitude—we must be praying, studying the Bible, worshiping, and engaging in whatever discipline we can because we love God and yearn to know Him better.

Elizabeth Cody Newenhuyse, a senior editor for *Moody Magazine*, says that we can get in the trap of doing the "right" things for the "wrong" reasons. "Defining 'how good a Christian' we are by how well we're performing is one way we warp the disciplines," she says. "Having a daily quiet time, or praying for hours, or reading three chapters of Scripture every day becomes the benchmark of our faith. This could be called 'practicing the presence of the practice' where doing the disciplines becomes an end in itself."

We must look to the disciplines, instead, as a meaningful and personal way to know our Savior in a more intimate way—know Him in the way that Hannah Whitall Smith did when she wrote, "He said such delightful things, that to find them out became my supreme delight." We can then move that growth in our relationship with Him outward and impact the world. Disciplines, in that way, can truly "change the world"—they can change our inner world and then, as a result, they can change the world around us because we are living in a way that communicates our love for Jesus Christ.

One point to remember as you read this book: it is not a definitive book. We have chosen some particular people who exemplify spiritual disciplines. We could have used the stories of so many more—both historical and contemporary—who changed the world and are continuing to change it by their consecrated lives.

This book has humbled us because the more we have studied spiritual practices, the more we have a deeper longing to practice them, and the more we are humbled that we had the privilege to write about them. We are motivated more than ever to put into practice everything we have learned and to "change the world" because of it.

May God use these disciplines to inspire you in the same way. May you have a desire to diligently and faithfully serve the Lord through the spiritual disciplines.

In doing so, you can change the world for God!

1
PRAYER

"It is not so true that 'prayer changes things' as that prayer changes me and I change things."—Oswald Chambers (1874–1917), devotional writer

"The prayer of the righteous is powerful and effective" (James 5:16 NRSV).

We parked and walked and then, suddenly, there was Ground Zero, six square blocks of twisted rubble, 110 floors of two imploded buildings, and their entire volume is less than two stories high," he said.

A week after the terrorist attacks on New York City's World Trade Center on September 11, 2001, Gordon and Gail McDonald traveled as Salvation Army volunteers to the area of destruction. Gordon's first impressions were of the massive devastation and the diligence of the rescue workers desperately trying to find survivors or locate bodies of victims.

Writing for *Leadership Journal*, Gordon said: "Then you notice the workmen, several thousand, like ants crawling over the pile, in bucket brigades of a hundred or more in a line. An unbroken line of workers was arriving, like soldiers to the front in a war. Each carried some kind of tool: a shovel, a pickax, electronic equipment. Another line, just as fascinating, but far more disturbing, was coming out. Men exhausted, filthy, hardly able to walk."

Gordon settled in at the Salvation Army work station and, as rescuers began walking out of the rubble, he and other volunteers handed out water. He also talked to them asking where they were from or if they knew anyone who was missing. He found that most men welcomed the chance to talk to anyone—even a stranger.

When the opportunity arose, Gordon would say, "I'm a guy who likes to pray for his friends. Would you mind a prayer?" Not one rescuer refused the offer—they were hungry for the support and prayer.

"Most reached out and grabbed my hand, or, if I put my hand on their shoulders, would come instinctively closer. My prayer was, "God, I thank You for my new friend. Please keep him brave, strong, safe, and true. And help him remember this city dearly loves him today."

Gordon continued to work at Ground Zero, distributing water, encouraging the workers, and praying with anyone who needed it. He says it was the most spiritually moving experience of his life. "No church service has spoken so deeply to my soul and witnessed to the presence of God as those hours at the crash site." The power of prayer broke through those moments of despair, providing rescuers with a sense of hope and encouragement. It has done the same thing for Christians throughout history.

One woman greatly influenced by the power of prayer was the famous Scottish missionary Mary Slessor (1848–1915). She once wrote: "My life is one long daily, hourly, record of answered prayer. For physical health, for mental overstrain, for guidance given marvelously . . . for food provided at the exact hour needed. . . . I can testify with a full and often wonder-stricken awe that I believe God answers prayer. I know God answers prayer. . . . It is the very atmosphere in which I live and breathe and have my being."

Our communion with God should be completely natural. It was to Mary. She spoke to God as a child to her Father when she needed help and strength or when her heart was filled with joy and gratitude. Prayer was what enabled Mary to face the dangers of the African bush. She believed in the reality of prayer because she had never found it to fail. During her many years of work in Calabar she faced chronic illness, loneliness, and fear. Opposing warring tribes, witchcraft, drunkenness, and superstition, the dauntless missionary finally won the respect of the tribes. She believed it was prayer that allowed her to do so.

When the Presbyterian missionary died on January 13, 1915, after four decades of sharing the gospel in Calabar, she was held in such high esteem that she was known as *Eka kpukpro Owo* (Mother of All the Peoples).

Both Mary Slessor and Gordon McDonald understood that prayer is one of the most important spiritual disciplines. It is through prayer that we have communion with God. Prayer brings us close to God, putting us directly in contact with Him.

Prayer is the key ingredient in a life that is pleasing to God and that glorifies God. It's of supreme importance, then, for our lives to be prayer-centered. When Jesus said to His disciples and to us, "And when you pray . . ." He assumed we would pray. It's a natural extension of our salvation and should be viewed as a necessary practice for our lives today. Our access to God's presence through prayer is possible because of Jesus.

Over the years, great men and women have written about the importance of the practice of prayer:

Protestant reformer Martin Luther (1483–1546) said, "To be a Christian without prayer is no more possible than to be alive without breathing."

William Law (1686–1761) in his classic *A Serious Call to a Devout and Holy Life* said, "Prayer is the nearest approach to God and the highest enjoyment of Him we can experience in this life."

E. M. Bounds (1835–1913) in his classic *Purpose in Prayer* said, "Prayer is the helpless and needy child crying to the compassion of the Father's heart and the bounty and power of a Father's hand."

Author Catherine Marshall in her book *Adventures in Prayer* said that prayer is asking: "Taking Jesus at His word that God really is our Father, in the most simple direct way, asking His help."

Prayer continues to be a priority for Christians who want to grow in their relationship with God. It is, therefore, one of the most essential disciplines for Christians to develop in their inner lives.

As physical exercise makes our bodies fit and strong, the spiritual exercise of prayer makes our entire being fit and strong for God's service.

Just as it's often difficult to get into a physical exercise routine, it can be challenging to make prayer a practical part of our lives. We must, though, make prayer a priority in our lives by asking ourselves: What are the keys to an effective prayer life? How do I attain success at prayer? How can I become a powerful pray-er?

We must first have a passion for Bible study, for the Bible teaches us about prayer. Then we have to obey what we read. Prayer and Bible study always go hand in hand.

Effective prayer is also dependent upon our right relationships with and treatment of other people (see Matt. 6:12,14–15; other teachings of Jesus; and numerous references in the Book of James).

We have to also daily cultivate a deep spiritual desire to pray fervently. To do that, we must understand that we are to pray in the Holy Spirit as Jude admonishes. "Dear friends, build yourselves up in your most holy faith and pray in the Holy Spirit" (Jude 1:20). As we submit ourselves to the guidance and teaching of the Holy Spirit, great results will come in our praying. Prayer involves surrender of our wills to God's, of what we want to what God wants. Those who pray in faith trust God and remain committed to Him even when He answers our prayers in ways other than we desire.

Also, we must realize that prayer takes strength. Hudson Taylor, founder of the China Inland Mission, understood that well. "Do not be so busy with work for Christ that you have no strength left for praying," he said. "True prayer requires strength."

Another way we can practice the discipline of prayer is to study the lives and writings of great men and women of God over the centuries who have changed the world; they all shared a commitment to prayer and Bible study. They believed God answers prayers; they lived in the will of God; they were persistent pray-ers. Their lives can inspire us today as we seek a deeper prayer life.

We can also learn from people today—writers, ministers, family members, friends, and neighbors who have discovered a deeper spiritual life through prayer.

THE WHEN, WHERE, AND HOW OF PRAYER

Becoming an effective pray-er usually doesn't happen overnight. We must determine the best way to incorporate it into our daily life—when, where, and how we will pray.

Time

We must find the time to pray. We can pray at any time—morning, noon, evening, or midnight. We can and should have a scheduled prayertime as well as pray during times of need or offer thanksgiving all during the day.

Jesus gave us some wonderful examples of finding time to pray. He prayed in the morning and at night. Mark records, "In the morning, while it was still very dark, he got up and went out to a deserted place, and there he prayed" (Mark 1:35). Luke says, "Jesus went out into the hills to pray and spent the night praying to God" (Luke 6:12).

We learn that King David prayed seven times a day. In Psalm 191:164 he said, "Seven times a day I praise you for your righteous laws."

Baptist missionary Adoniram Judson's practice was to devote two or three hours each day to prayer. Like King David, he withdrew seven times a day—at dawn, then at 9:00, 12:00, 3:00, 6:00, 9:00, and midnight. The first great American missionary hero, Judson had a prayer life which enabled him to translate the Bible into Burmese, produce a dictionary, and train many pastors and evangelists.

When Becky Tirabassi, best-selling Christian author and founder of the Change Your Life ministry, attended a conference for youth workers she learned that prayer was not a priority in her life—but that it needed to be.

One speaker after another at the conference talked about the importance and power of prayer. When the weekend's closing workshop also focused on prayer, Becky knew that God was speaking directly to her. She knew she had to make some big changes in her prayer life. She went home with a new conviction, and a plan.

"An hour a day," she decided. "I had to take a radical step closer to God. I took the plunge and left the conference, bathed afresh in the power of the Holy Spirit."

Becky's busy schedule and cluttered life made the plan difficult to implement ("Little did I know what I was asking for when I made a simple decision to pray for an hour each day!"), but it soon became the most powerful part of her schedule.

Of the lessons she learned, Becky says: "In my daily hour of quiet time with the Lord, a new strength was developing. I would encounter God in a new way, discover something fresh about His character daily, and receive a boldness to believe Him for more and more power in my life. Hour after hour revealed that God was not just real or just alive, but intimately involved and interested in every aspect of my life."

Martin Luther had a similar prayer plan. "If I fail to spend two hours in prayer each morning, the devil gets the victory through the day. I have so much business I cannot get on without spending three hours daily in prayer."

We must take the time to listen to God and set aside specific time to do so. Author and workshop leader Jennifer Kennedy Dean says, "If I am sure that nothing else matters as much as spending time fully absorbed in Him, then nothing will distract me from that pursuit."

Our time with God is a gift we give to Him. It is the least we can do for Him because of all He has done for us.

Place

We can pray anywhere.

Jesus prayed many places: on the mountains (Matt. 14:23, Mark 6:46, John 6:15, and Luke 9:28); at His baptism (Luke 3:21); in the garden before his arrest (Luke 22:41).

Evelyn Christenson, in her best-selling book What *Happens When Women Pray*, says that we should go each day to our particular "prayer closet." In addition, she adds that we can make wherever we are a prayer closet. She says, "I have found another kind of closet praying. It's just drawing apart to God wherever I am—at the kitchen sink, at a desk, or even in a room filled with people."

Many people like to go to the same place every day for their daily concentrated prayertime. That way they can have their Bible, pen, prayer journal, devotional book, etc., easily at their disposal. Jennifer K. Dean says that "going to the same place immediately causes me to transition from outward focus to inward focus because that place has become my altar or my sanctuary. My heart is trained by practice to bow down in that place."

Position

We can pray in any position. We can pray on our knees or bending over in our garden. We can pray while driving in our car or standing in church.

Jesus in the garden of Gethsemane prayed kneeling (Luke 22:41); at the tomb of Lazarus He "lifted up His eyes" (John 11:41).

"Most often, I sit quietly in my chair and assume a worship posture mentally, in the inner sanctuary of my soul," Jennifer says. "However, there are times when I bodily, physically fall on my face or stand with my hands lifted. Or even—dare I admit it?—dance in His presence. Sometimes the pleasure of His presence is so great that my joy spills over into physical expression."

Method

When we pray, we should find a technique that is reverent, worshipful, and comfortable to us.

We can pray with our eyes open or shut. We can pray aloud or silently, write our prayers in our journal, or sing our prayers. We can pray prescribed prayers—the Lord's Prayer, other pieces of Scripture, or we can express our own prayers.

Mother Teresa (1910–1997) said, "I always begin my prayer in silence, for it is in the silence of the heart that God speaks."

COMPONENTS OF PRAYER

Prayer consists of a number of elements. One of the most effective formulas for prayer is the ACTS system—Adoration, Confession, Thanksgiving, and Supplication.

Adoration

We should spend much time thinking about God and adoring—loving and worshiping—Him. We should focus on the glory and majesty of God.

Author Evelyn Underhill (1875–1941) insightfully wrote: "It is only through adoration and attention that we make our personal discoveries about him. . . . I think that if you have only as little as half an hour to give each morning to your private prayer, it is not too much to make up your minds to spend half that time in such adoration. . . . Its neglect is responsible for much lack of spiritual depth and power.

"In the flood tide of such adoring prayer, the soul is released from the strife and confusions of temporal life; it is lifted far beyond all petty controversies, petty worries and vanities—and none of us escapes these things. It is carried into God, hidden in him."

Confession

We need to confess our sins daily—admit and acknowledge them—so we will have an effective intercessory prayer life. Instead of generally confessing our sins, we should specifically name them and confess them. In doing so, our spirit will be lightened, and we will be more open to the guidance and reassurance God will give to us.

The Bible tells us that God wants us to have a broken spirit before Him. "A broken and a contrite heart, O God, thou wilt not despise" (Psalm 51:17).

John says, "If we confess our sins, he who is faithful and just will forgive us our sins and cleanse us from all unrighteousness" (1 John 1:9).

English poet Christina G. Rossetti (1830–1894) said, "Though our sins be seven, though our sins be seventy times seven, though our sins be more in number than the hairs of our head, yet give us grace in loving penitence to cast ourselves down into the depth of Thy compassion."

Thanksgiving

Thanksgiving is a vital part of our praying. When we are thankful, God's power is unleashed in our lives and the "peace of God, which transcends all understanding" (Phil. 4:7) comes into our lives.

The psalmist gave thanks to God: "O give thanks to the Lord, call on his name" (Psalm 105:1).

The Apostle Paul said, "Do not be anxious about anything, but in everything, by prayer and petition, with thanksgiving, present your requests to God" (Phil. 4:6).

Paul taught us how to give thanks: "Giving thanks to God the Father at all times and for everything in the name of our Lord Jesus Christ" (Eph. 5:20).

Have a grateful heart even when you don't feel like it. God will give you His perfect peace and healing when you are thankful.

Supplication

In supplication we are humbly and earnestly making our petitions known to God.

What does the Bible say that we should pray for? In the Lord's Prayer, Jesus said to pray for our daily needs (Matt. 6:11), forgiveness (Matt. 6:12), and protection from temptation (Matt. 6:12). James says we are to pray for wisdom (James 1:5).

Paul's writings remind us of other things to pray for: growth in spiritual understanding (Eph. 1:17–19) and opportunities to tell others about Jesus (Col. 4:3–5).

James tells us to pray when we are in trouble (James 5:13). This clearly is a directive to pray for ourselves when we are suffering.

The Bible tells us to pray for others through intercessory prayer. It says, "First of all, then, I urge that supplications, prayers, intercessions, and thanksgivings be made for everyone" (1 Tim. 2:1 NRSV). We should pray for our spouses, children, relatives, fellow Christians, and unbelievers.

Writer Jane Ann Clark says that her Aunt Wanda taught her the importance of praying for others. She remembers waking up one summer night in the wee hours of the morning; Jane Ann was just 10 years old. She heard a voice softly speaking and saw a light filtering into her room from down the hall. She tiptoed down the hall and peeked around the door into Aunt Wanda's bedroom. Her aunt sat in the middle of her big four-poster bed, photographs scattered in front of her and a map of the world spread beside her.

Jane Ann remembers: "I watched from my hiding place as she lovingly touched each photo, praying for the family member or friend pictured there. She prayed for guidance for her nephew as he finished college and searched for the job that would best serve God. She prayed for strength and comfort for her sister whose husband had died of a heart attack. She prayed for a wayward brother. On and on she prayed for each personal need."

She then moved on to the world map. "She prayed for different countries as she traced the outline of that country with her fingertip," she says. "She prayed for the missionaries working there and the people who would hear the word of God."

Jane Ann says that night changed her forever. "Whenever I strayed away from God, I'd see Aunt Wanda touching my old school picture and calling out my name to God," she says. "And now, years later, my family's pictures are becoming worn from my fingerprints and, of course, I have a big tattered map of the world."

Paul wrote to the Corinthians about praying for him: "On him we have set our hope that he will continue to deliver us, as you help us by your prayers" (2 Cor. 1:10–11).

Oswald Chambers said, "The real business of your life as a saved soul is intercessory prayer. Wherever God puts you in circumstances, pray immediately, pray that His Atonement may be realized in other lives. . . . Pray for your friends now; pray for those with whom you come in contact now."

PRAY BELIEVING

We need to have a strong resolve to not give up in intercessory prayer. We are not to let disappointment or impatience keep us from praying for others. We should remember that as we pray God fights the battle.

St. Augustine (354–430) wrote in his *Confessions* that "almost nine years passed, in which I wallowed in . . . the darkness of falsehood." He said all that time his mother, Monica, "ceased not at all hours her devotions to bewail my case unto Thee." In 387 St. Augustine turned from his wicked ways and surrendered his life to Jesus. His mother's work completed—her fervent prayers answered—she died in a few months.

We must always hold fast to the belief that God will answer our prayers—even if we don't see immediate responses. Pray, always believing. In the New Testament we read, "If you believe, you will receive whatever you ask for in prayer" (Matt. 21:22).

“When there is a matter that requires definite prayer, pray till you believe God, until with unfeigned lips you can thank Him for the answer,” said Lettie B. Cowman (1870–1960), author of the classic *Streams in the Desert.*

PRAY IN THE SPIRIT

We must always be alert for the Holy Spirit's guidance toward prayer. When we feel God nudging us to pray, we should respond in obedience.

Marilynn Blackaby remembers a Sunday afternoon when she felt guided by the Holy Spirit to pray for her three sons, who were traveling a long distance. “As I washed dishes, I was talking to the Lord because I knew it was about the time the boys would be heading home on a narrow two-lane road. Suddenly, I knew the Lord wanted me to pray for my kids,” she recalls.

She ran to wake up her husband, Henry (author of the best-selling *Experiencing God* Bible study), who was napping. She told him, “Down on your knees. We need to pray for the boys. We prayed and prayed until I sensed everything was all right.”

When their sons arrived home, they told of a near-disastrous accident as their car hit some black ice and spun out of control. They almost hit an 18-wheeler. “Of course, you know what time that was—right when Henry and I were praying for them.”

Sometimes we have a difficult time voicing our prayers, but the Holy Spirit comes to our aid. The Bible tells us: “We do not know what we ought to pray, but the Spirit himself intercedes for us with groans that words cannot express” (Rom. 8:26). Author Joni Eareckson Tada put it well. “I'm so glad that God can read my heart and understand what's going on even when I am handicapped by my own weakness or words.”

The Apostle Paul gave us more direction about the role of the Holy Spirit in prayer: “And pray in the Spirit on all occasions with all kinds of prayers and requests. With this in mind, be alert and always keep on praying for all the saints” (Eph. 6:18).

Hearing the Holy Spirit's guidance only happens when we are actively listening to God. Mother Teresa knew the importance of keeping our ears open for God's voice. She said, "We need to listen to God because it's not what we say but what He says to us and through us that matters. . . . As blood is to the body, prayer is to the soul, and it brings you closer to God."

FAITHFUL IN PRAYER

We should be faithful in praying for people. If we say we are going to pray, we should. In 1 Samuel 12:23 we read, "God forbid that I should sin against the Lord in ceasing to pray for you."

Paul emphasized the importance of faithfulness in our prayers. In Ephesians 6:18, he said, "Pray in the Spirit on all occasions with all kinds of prayers and requests. With this in mind, be alert and always keep on praying for all the saints."

We should also be persistent in our prayers. In Luke 18:1–8, Jesus told His disciples a parable about the persistent widow that illustrated that "they should always pray and not give up." Paul said in Colossians 4:2, "Be persistent in prayer." In 1 Thessalonians 5:17, Paul states, "Pray without ceasing."

Protestant reformer Martin Luther (1483–1546) focused on the words of the Apostle Paul when he said: "Upright Christians pray without ceasing; though they pray not always with their mouths, but their hearts pray continually, sleeping and waking; for the sigh of a true Christian is a prayer."

Dwight and Lila Reagan, missionaries in South Africa, know about persisting in prayer. For 17 years, they witnessed to and prayed for the salvation of a Hindu woman. In one of their missionary letters home they wrote, "While she was terribly ill, she called her daughter (who is a Christian) into her bedroom. She said, 'It is time.' 'Time for what, Mother?' 'It is time that I accepted Jesus as my Savior.' We prayed and worked and loved this woman for all those years, and she finally accepted Him!"

ANSWERED PRAYERS

Oswald Chambers perceptively said, "Jesus never mentioned unanswered prayer, he had the boundless certainty that prayer is always answered."

Chambers understood the words of Jesus: "When you pray, go into your room, close the door and pray to your Father, who is unseen. Then your Father, who sees what is done in secret, will reward you" (Matt. 6:6).

After his death two ridges, or grooves, were discovered in the wooden floor by George Mueller's (1805–1898) bed. Kneeling to pray, he had literally worn two depressions into the floor.

Born in Prussia, he was converted at a prayer meeting at the age of 20. He moved to London in 1829 and joined the Plymouth Brethren movement. When he began his first pastorate at Ebenezer Chapel, he took no salary and began his life of trust and faith for his needs. While pastoring a church in Bristol in 1834, he founded the Scriptural Knowledge Institution for Home and Abroad which promoted education of biblical principles, circulated Scriptures, and supported missionary work.

He opened his first orphans home in 1835. Beginning with only two shingles (50 cents) and a few orphans, he eventually housed and educated 2,000 children in five houses on Ashley Down near Bristol. He never asked for money. Yet, in response to his powerful prayer and faith, God sent over $7 million.

When he was 70, he and his wife set out on a worldwide missionary tour which lasted for 17 years and led to the establishment of orphanages based on his faith principles.

Displaying his unwavering faith in God, he once wrote, "I am no longer anxious about anything . . . for he, I know, is able to carry out his will, and his will is mine. It makes no matter where he places me, or how."

Like Mueller, J. Hudson Taylor (1832–1905), was a great man of prayer. One of the most outstanding missionary statesmen the world has ever known, he founded the China Inland Mission (CIM; now called Overseas Missionary Fellowship) which became the model for interdenominational "faith" missions.

Taylor left Liverpool, England, on September 19, 1853, and arrived at Woosung, China, on March 1, 1854. The next 6 years found him journeying inland preaching and depending totally upon God to meet his needs. One of the lessons he learned he later taught others: "Depend upon it. God's work, done in God's way, will never lack for supplies."

He and his wife, Maria, whom he married in 1858, returned to England in 1860. During the next 5 years he translated the Bible into the Ningpo dialect and completed his medical training. On June 25, 1865, the idea of CIM was born. On May 26, 1866, the Taylors sailed for China with 17 missionary recruits.

At Taylor's death, CIM had 205 mission stations, 849 missionaries, and an estimated 125,000 Chinese Christians.

Missionary Amy Carmichael (1867–1951) also believed that prayer was at the heart of her mission. She believed that God answered her prayers and that He would send her the right people for her ministry in India. In her letters back home to Ireland she listed "prayer first, last, and always."

Amy established a day of prayer on the sixth day of every month to intercede for her Hindu children. "We remembered a time of threatened famine, when prices were suddenly rising and 20 pounds were needed to lay in a stock of paddy (unshelled rice)," she said. "That week brought us a single gift of 20 pounds from a friend in England, whose very name up to that time was unknown to us."

The great literary missionary Frank Laubach (1884–1970) remarked about people praying for him: "I am very sensitive and know whether you are praying for me. If one of you lets me down, I feel it. When you are praying for me, I feel a strange power." Sustained by fervent prayer, Frank touched 100 million people through his visionary literacy program—Each One Teach One. This method involved a nonreader who learned to read teaching another nonreader to read.

MEDITATION AND PRAYER

If we acknowledge that prayer involves not just talking to God, but listening for Him, we will realize that meditation is an integral ingredient.

For Luci Swindoll, an author and member of the Women of Faith tour, that means finding time for silent reflection with God. "When I want to completely retreat to the quiet life, it's not with my friends, the crickets, or the bath. It's with the Lord," she says. "Talk about a balm to my spirit. The joy and pleasure of speaking with the Lord is far superior to anything life on this earth affords. Through prayer I become centered and serene. When it's quiet and still, I sense the Lord comes near as I enter His presence."

Luci says that we should remember the story of Mary and Martha in the Gospel of Luke; it gives us some wonderful insight into the role of quiet meditation with the Lord. Martha was busy running around, preparing for Jesus' visit. When Jesus saw her fretting about making everything "just right," He told her, "Martha, Martha . . . you are worried and upset about many things, but only one thing is needed. Mary has chosen what is better" (Luke 10:41–42). Luci says we can learn from this story because "we know what Mary was doing: sitting calmly, quietly, at the Master's feet."

Thomas à Kempis (1379?–1471) said in the classic *The Imitation of Christ*, "Seek a suitable time for thy meditation, and think frequently of the mercies of God to thee."

Meditation is an old discipline. Old Testament prophets practiced it; David often sat in his shepherd's field and spent hours meditating and then writing beautiful songs about it.

St. Augustine (354-430) wrote his spiritual autobiography, *The Confessions of St. Augustine*, in 397. In this classic devotional meditation, he records his search for the truth about God and himself. The great spiritual mystics Teresa of Avila and Madame Guyon were also known for their meditation.

One of the best verses for Christian meditation is Philippians 4:8: "Whatsoever things are true, whatsoever things are honest, whatsoever things are just, whatsoever things are pure, whatsoever things are lovely, whatsoever things are of good report; if there be any virtue, and if there be any praise, think on these things."

FASTING

Fasting involves going without food for the purpose of spending more time for spiritual pursuits.

Pastor John Simmons believes that fasting is a highly effective way to make prayer more meaningful. He has fasted many times over the years, but points to one time when he, his wife, and daughter all fasted together. His wife and daughter fasted for seven days; he fasted for ten.

"I fasted for guidance specifically related to some things going on in my church at the time," John said. "It's a powerful way to get connected with God and to revive yourself spiritually."

John's fast allowed for nothing except liquids, but he stresses that Christians can fast in different ways. "You can fast for a day, or fast for a meal," he said. "During Lent, I encourage church members to fast from an activity that keeps them separated from God."

He says that all fasting should be surrounded by prayer. "You pray for specific concerns while you fast," he says. "And you also use prayer when you feel a hunger pang or feel like you can't go on."

John believes that fasting is the most neglected of spiritual disciplines today. "Christians today don't appreciate fasting," he says, "but it's a wonderful discipline to practice."

TYPES OF PRAYER

The familiar image of praying is often one of either a church praying corporately or an individual praying alone. There are other ways, though, that praying can be utilized in a spiritually effective way. Prayer vigils, prayerwalking, praying the Bible—these are just a few examples.

Prayer Vigils, Services, and Marches

The United States and the world united in prayer following the September 11, 2001, terrorist attacks on New York City and Washington, D. C.; this often came in the form of prayer services, marches, and vigils.

The America Prays vigil involved nearly 1,300 churches; 13,000 Promise Keepers in San Jose, California; a live simulcast for TV and radio; and a Web cast on Crosswalk.com. Others were sponsored by individual churches and communities. The vigils showed the power of praying together—lifting up prayers together before the throne of God.

Prayerwalking

Prayerwalking has been defined as "praying on-site with insight." It involves walking through neighborhoods or communities with the intent of praying for individuals or families in homes, schools, and places of business.

Praying the Bible

An effective way to pray—perhaps when you can't summon the words on your own, or when you want to pray for a particular reason—is to pray the Bible.

Popular author Beth Moore has dedicated an entire book to praying the Bible. The book, called *Praying God's Word*, encourages Christians to pray Scriptures in order to overcome strongholds they may be facing in their lives. Beth says she has an "unquenchable desire to share one of the most effective approaches to the liberated life in Christ that God has ever taught me: praying Scripture to overcome strongholds."

She recommends reading specific Bible verses and passages daily in order to get through struggles and to grow as a Christian. She says that the combination of prayer and God's Word is amazingly effective; she compares the combination to two sticks of dynamite—separate they are strong, but together they are unbelievably powerful!

There are a number of Bible passages that are effective for praying. Two meaningful ones to pray are Matthew 6:33: "But seek first his kingdom and his righteousness, and all these things will be given to you as well"; and Galatians 5:22: "The fruit of the Spirit is love, joy, peace, patience, kindness, goodness, faithfulness, gentleness, and self-control."

Some Christians pray the Great Commission to inspire and encourage them to be better witnesses for Christ. In Matthew 28:19–20 Jesus said, "Therefore, go and make disciples of all nations, baptizing them in the name of the Father and of the Son and of the Holy Spirit, and teaching them to obey everything I have commanded you. And surely I am with you always to the very end of the age."

And the most famous of all prayers is the Lord's Prayer, found in Matthew 6:9: "Our Father in heaven, hallowed be your name, your kingdom come, your will be done on earth as it is in heaven. Give us today our daily bread. Forgive us our debts, as we also forgive our debtors. And lead us not into temptation, but deliver us from evil."

When Todd Beamer found himself a victim of hijackers on United Airlines Flight 93 on September 11, 2001, he relied on his faith during his last moments alive. In a conversation with a GTE Airfone operator about the hijacking, he recited the Lord's Prayer and then told the woman that he and other passengers were going to attempt to thwart the terrorists. Todd's pastor had recently preached a series of sermons on the Lord's Prayer, and Todd relied on prayer daily.

Flash Prayers

Literacy missionary Frank Laubach developed an idea called flash prayers where he proposed that we pray "swishing prayers" at everyone we meet. This practice keeps us in a constant state of prayer.

Jennifer Kennedy Dean puts it this way: "When you come to understand that prayer is not just the words you sandwich between "Dear God" and "Amen," but is a flow of His provision and His powerful, active presence in your life, 'praying continually' makes more sense. The more you learn to be aware of Him, the more you understand that every thought becomes a prayer. Every conversation becomes a prayerful expression. Every situation becomes a platform for His power. Prayer is the way your soul breathes.

"Prayer is not a duty you perform for God. You are praying even when you are not forming your thoughts into sentences. You can always be engaged in prayer, the interchange of love between you and the Father," she says.

Breath Prayers

Breath prayers are brief personalized prayers relevant and meaningful to an individual. By choosing a personal breath prayer—such as "God,

You are holy"; "Lord, give me strength"—you have a prayer you can recite at any moment during the day. Use your breath prayer to strengthen or encourage you, or to remind you of God's amazing grace in your life.

In Matthew 6:7–8 Jesus said, "And when you pray, do not keep on babbling like pagans, for they think they will be heard because of their many words. Do not be like them, for your Father knows what you need before you ask Him."

Praying in Cyberspace

The Internet has changed the way we communicate with others. It has also added a new dimension to praying.

Christians today use the Internet to post prayer requests, join online prayer groups, and circulate prayers by email. Missionaries around the world use the Internet to share their stories, requests, and answered prayers.

JOY OF PRAYER

However we utilize the methods of prayer—whether we are fasting and praying; meditating and praying; participating in a prayer vigil; prayerwalking; or attending a prayer retreat—it should be a joyful experience. There should be much joy in the experience of getting close to and communing with our God.

Missionary leader A. B. Simpson (1844–1919) put it so well: "It is the joy of prayer, this joy of the Lord. Its element is the secluded prayer room, and its source is the mercy seat. No prayerless life can be a happy one."

PERSONAL QUESTIONS ABOUT PRAYER

- Will I discipline myself to be a person of prayer?
- Will I commit to pray daily for others?
- Am I experiencing the joy of answered prayer?
- Will I persist to pray even when my prayers don't seem to be answered?

- Will I pray confidently that my prayers will be answered?
- Am I depending on God completely to meet all my needs?

MAKING PRAYER PART OF YOUR LIFE

- Whether you have been praying for decades or just started a prayer life, ask God to give you a deeper desire to pray.
- Choose a favorite place to pray. Go there each day at the same time.
- Make listening to God an important part of your praying. Be quiet and wait for His guidance.
- Keep a prayer journal. Write down your prayers and your answers to prayers.
- If you tell someone that you will pray for him or her, do not neglect that commitment you have made.
- Spend time earnestly praying—for a friend in need, a missionary, a family member, and victims of terrorist attacks in the US and around the world.
- Pray for those who daily are persecuted for their faith around the world.
- Pray daily about a sinful habit that you need help from God to overcome.
- Study prayers found in the Bible.
- Pray the Lord's Prayer slowly meditating on each phrase.
- Open up to God. Talk to Him as you would a friend or a parent. Thank Him for His gifts; spend time in adoration. Tell Him your worries; ask for guidance.
- Get involved in the prayer ministry of your church. If your church doesn't have a prayer room, consider speaking to your pastor about designating a room for prayer.
- Meditate. Pray before you meditate, voice meditations, or silently meditate. Write meditations in a journal.
- Try different approaches to prayer. For example, prayerwalk. Walk down your street praying for each family and their specific needs.
- Pray breath prayers as you walk or drive in your car. Example: "Praise God from whom all blessing flow"; or "Speak, Lord, Your servant is listening."

• As you read your newspaper today, pray for people in your town: those grieving, those in the hospital, those in prison, those who are victims of crime, etc.
• Pray daily for the President and other national leaders.
• Get involved the first Thursday in May with the National Day of Prayer activities in your city.
• Purchase a book on prayer or check out one from your church media library.

APPLICATION VERSE

"Do not be anxious about anything, but in everything, by prayer and petition, with thanksgiving, present your requests to God. And the peace of God which transcends all understanding, will guard your hearts and minds in Christ Jesus" (Phil. 4:6–7).

PRAYER

Thank You, God, for the privilege of prayer, that we can pray to the Lord of the universe and that You welcome our prayers. Give me a yearning to pray fervently and persistently believing that You will answer my prayers. Amen.

2
Bible Study

"I never knew all there was in the Bible until I spent those years in jail. I was constantly finding new treasures."—John Bunyan (1618–1688), author of more than 60 books including the classic *Pilgrim's Progress*

"Open my eyes that I may see wonderful things in your law" (Psalm 119:18).

In 1952 in San Bernardino, California, Audrey Wetherell Johnson was asked to teach the Bible to five women who were already familiar with the Bible. She questioned why she was being asked to give more to those who already had so much. She had for years been teaching the Bible to people who knew nothing about it. She found the answer in biblical passages such as Zechariah 4:10: "'Who despises the day of small things?'" Maybe it was not such a small thing for her to teach the women.

Johnson (1907–1984) always went to the Bible for answers. Born in England, she became a Christian as she studied these words of Jesus: "'Whoever lives and believes in me will never die. Do you believe this?'" (John 11:26). She became deeply committed to the authority of the Scripture. She not only believed it, but she taught it and lived it all of her life. In 1936 she went to China as a missionary with the China Inland Mission. In 1942, after the Japanese invasion, she was interned in a camp in huts that had formerly been horse stables. She remained faithful to God although suffering under incredibly harsh conditions. She returned to England following the war but was back teaching at the China Bible Seminary in Shanghai in 1947. After the Communists put her under house arrest in 1948, she was forced to leave in 1950. That is when she found herself in California confronted with teaching the Bible to five women.

She threw herself into this new task. She adopted a few simple questions for the women: "(l) What does the passage say? (2) What did it mean to the people in the day it was written? (3) What does it mean to me?" This was the beginning of what became Bible Study Fellowship (BSF), developing into five series of studies, each 32 weeks in duration, which deal with almost the entire Bible. BSF was incorporated in Oakland, California, in 1958 and soon grew to almost 300 classes with 100,000 members. The headquarters moved to San Antonio, Texas, in 1980; 4 years later Miss J., as she was affectionately called, died. She left a legacy of disciplined and personal Bible study with an application to everyday living. Today BSF International reaches out to men and women everywhere.

Technical writer Carolyn Life studied under BSF while she lived in San Antonio in 1982 and 1983. When she moved to Huntsville, Alabama, in 1986, she joined a BSF group there. Her most productive time of spiritual growth, she says, came as a member and discussion leader. "Serving in that capacity was my joy for 4 years. The in-depth study and personal insight gained by following the disciplined approach of the BSF material was invaluable to me," she remembers.

Carolyn's involvement in the Bible study helped her in many different ways over the years. The discipline she gained aided her when she returned to college as an adult student. It also helped her in understanding the community of Christ.

"The interaction with other Christian women from various Protestant denominations and Catholic churches in our area was wonderful," Carolyn says. "The friendships we developed and the prayers we shared were a constant blessing. When my husband died suddenly, their support, prayers, and love were lifesaving to me."

Bible study is integral to our growth as Christians; it is one of the most essential of all the spiritual disciplines. We can engage in Bible study in various ways—personally, with our families, in Sunday School classes at church, in community groups such as BSF, and in other church Bible study groups. Bible study is essential to our spiritual growth because it provides the way that we can get to know our Lord.

AN ESSENTIAL BOOK

The Bible is the greatest book ever written, the best-seller of all time. It is a source of wisdom, strength, steadfastness, encouragement, peace, joy, and hope to millions.

The Bible fulfills so many roles in our lives. It is:

Our spiritual food. The Bible is the Christian's spiritual nourishment. In order for our inner life to grow and be strong, we need to feast upon God's written Word. Jesus said, "'It is written: "One does not live by bread alone, but by every word that comes from the mouth of God"'" (Matt. 4:4 NRSV). And Luke 11:28 records Jesus as saying, "'Blessed rather are those who hear the word of God and obey it.'"

Our standard. The Bible's teachings are the supreme standards by which we should evaluate everything. "Every word of God proves true," asserted the writer of Proverbs (Prov. 30:5 NRSV); and Isaiah proclaimed, "The grass withers, the flower fades; but the word of our God will stand forever" (Isa. 40:8 NRSV).

Shaper of our lives. Reading and meditating on the Bible shapes our thoughts, attitudes, and actions. As Paul said to Timothy, "Do your best to present yourself to God as one approved by him, a worker who has no need to be ashamed, rightly explaining the word of truth" (2 Tim. 2:15 NRSV). The writer of Hebrews said, "For the word of God is living and active. Sharper than any double-edged sword, it penetrates even to dividing soul and spirit, joints and marrow; it judges the thoughts and attitudes of the heart " (Heb. 4:12).

Our knowledge of God. "Long ago God spoke to our ancestors in many and various ways by the prophets," according to the writer of Hebrews, "but in these last days he has spoken to us by a Son, whom he appointed the heir of all things, through whom he also created the world" (Heb. 1:1–2 NRSV). The Old Testament teaches us how God revealed himself to the Hebrew people by calling Abraham and through him made a covenant to bless all people on earth. And we learn how God spoke to the prophets declaring through them the coming of the Messiah.

Our guide to salvation. The Bible shows the way to salvation through faith in Jesus. The Old Testament pointed to Jesus. The New Testament gives us the plan of salvation and tells about the transformed lives of those who believed. Paul told Timothy that Scripture leads us to salvation: "Continue in what you have learned and have become convinced of, because you know those from whom you learned it, and how from infancy you have known the holy Scriptures, which are able to make you wise for salvation through faith in Christ Jesus" (2 Tim. 3:14–15).

Our tool for witnessing. Once we have experienced salvation, the New Testament teaches over and over that we are to take the gospel to others. Jesus in the parable of the sower said that the "good soil represents honest, good-hearted people. They listen to God's words and cling to them and steadily spread them to others who also soon believe" (Luke 8:15 TLB).

Our divine instruction. The Bible is a perfect treasure of divine instruction. Paul said that it is the basis for sound doctrine, useful for exposing errors of false teaching and doctrine, guides us to righteous living, and equips us for service: "All scripture is inspired by God and is useful for teaching, for reproof, for correction, and for training in righteousness, so that everyone who belongs to God may be proficient, equipped for every good work" (2 Tim. 3:16–17 NRSV).

Our hope for the present and future. "For everything that was written in the past was written to teach us," Paul wrote, "so that through endurance and the encouragement of the Scriptures we might have hope" (Rom. 15:4). The Bible provides us with the hope we need to face uncertainty with faith and courage.

Essential to live the abundant life. A serious study of the Bible is essential for every Christian to grow and live the abundant life. "If we are to be Christians whose hearts beat and break with the rhythm of the heart of God," says Charles Colson, "we must take on his whole Word wholeheartedly." While the Word of God is not confined just to the Bible—Jesus is God's Living Word, for example—the Bible is a primary source for God's words to us.

A PRECIOUS BOOK

We often take the Bible for granted. We should never forget, though, how many people died so we could have the privilege of reading and studying it. In 1526 William Tyndale published his English translation of the New Testament. Ten years later he was burned at the stake because of his translation and distribution of the New Testament.

Many Protestants were killed simply because they read the Bible and shared the Word with others. One such man was Englishman George Wishart, a professor at the University of Cambridge. In 1543 he was burned at the stake for heresy. Before his death he said, "I exhort you to love the Word of God and suffer patiently, with a comfortable heart, for the sake of the Word, which is your salvation and everlasting comfort."

People continue to be martyred throughout the world today for studying the Bible.

Romulo Saune worked for years to translate the Bible into Quechua-Ayachucho, the language of his native people in Peru. In 1992 Romulo and three other Christians brought food, clothes, the Bible, and New Testaments to the village of Chakiqpampa. He preached to the village and 28 people trusted in Jesus.

As they left the town, rejoicing in the wonderful time of fellowship they had, they were stopped by Marxist soldiers. With guns pointed at him, Romulo told the men: "God loves you and I love you"; he went on to share the gospel with them. Moments later, though, a leader of the terrorist group shot the four men dead. Witnesses of the killing say that Romulo's final words were "God, I love You! Jesus, I love You!"

Countless people around the world today long for their own copy of the Bible and treasure the Bible when they finally receive one. John Ward, a circuit judge in Fort Smith, Arkansas, and a member of Gideons International, met a man in Indonesia who travels 18 hours by boat three times a year to load up Bibles and carry them to his area.

BIBLE ILLITERACY

While many people around the world yearn to have their own Bibles, copies are readily found in most people's homes in America. Often, though, it is the most neglected book in the home. About 92 percent of Americans own at least 1 Bible; the average household has 3 Bibles.

Two-thirds of Americans say it holds the answers to the basic questions of life. Everyone wants to read the Bible, but few do. A November 2000 Gallup poll showed that the number of people who read the Bible occasionally has dropped to 59 percent from 73 percent in the 1980s.

Another recent Gallup survey shows, though, that fewer than half of Americans can name the first book of the Bible, one-third know who delivered the Sermon the Mount, and one-quarter don't know why we celebrate Easter.

At least 20 million Bibles are sold each year; tens of millions are distributed free, but Bible reading is declining. As George W. Gallup, the nation's foremost religion pollster, said, "We revere the Bible, but we don't read it."

Why? According to a survey by Tyndale House Publishers, 64 percent of Americans don't read it because they're too busy. The daunting size of the Bible is another reason.

A modest, unassuming businessman from Lansing, Michigan, has been combating biblical illiteracy since 1976.

That year W. James Russell and his wife, Phyllis, founded the Amy Foundation (named after their daughter). Russell says, "Although the value system of the United States and Western civilization is based on the Judeo-Christian ethic, surveys indicate fewer than 17 percent of the American people read the Bible regularly. We are trying to sustain a value system with little or no knowledge of the historically proven truths of our biblically established value system.

"The Amy Award was designed to encourage writers to do the necessary research to rediscover, understand, and communicate the character building truths forming the foundation of our value system." In order to do that, the Amy Writing Awards invite writers to communicate biblical truth to a secular audience. Cash awards of $34,000 are given each year to 15 winners.

In addition to the writing awards, the foundation has a Discipled Nation Plan, an effort to disciple the nation by 2025; the Amy Internet Syndicate, serving 1,500 daily and 10,000 community newspapers; church writing groups all over the country that teach how to present biblical truth in local mainstream media; a monthly newsletter, "Pen &

Sword"; and an abundance of discipling resources. Their Web site at www.amyfound.org contains more information.

COMMITMENT TO READ THE BIBLE

We know the Bible is important (Gallup's results show that even non-Christians recognize that fact), yet we often stay uncommitted to reading and studying it on a regular basis. To grow as believers, and to change the world around us, we must change that attitude. We must become committed to Bible study.

Tim LaHaye in *How to Study the Bible for Yourself* says, "There is only one possible way to grow strong spiritually—reading and studying the Word of God." As individual believers, we must make a commitment to read, study, and meditate on God's Holy Word and to pass the tradition of Bible reading on to our children and grandchildren. As Moses said in Deuteronomy 6:7 (NRSV) about God's commandments: "Recite them to your children and talk about them when you are at home and when you are away, when you lie down and when you rise." We will go a long way in increasing Bible literacy overall by starting with ourselves!

Effective Christians are students of the Bible. They know the value in reading and searching the Bible for instruction, inspiration, and guidance.

PREPARATION FOR BIBLE STUDY

You may be like so many people who say, "I want to become a better student of the Bible. How do I get started?"

The first step is prayer. Pray for God to speak to you as you study the Bible. Ask the Holy Spirit to help you first to understand what the passage is saying and then apply what you read to your life. Remember that people wrote under the inspiration of the Holy Spirit. The Holy Spirit guided them to preserve and translate the Bible. We receive the message of the Bible through the Holy Spirit.

Approach Bible study with a teachable mind. Paul wrote to Timothy, "Reflect on what I am saying, for the Lord will give you insight into all this" (2 Tim. 2:7); and to the Ephesians he wrote, "I keep asking that the God of our Lord Jesus Christ, the glorious Father, may give you the Spirit of wisdom and revelation, so that you may know him better" (Eph. 1:17).

Look at the Scriptures with an open mind and open heart. Allow God to reveal to you the things you need to know.

Missionary A. B. Simpson said, "We need new eyes with which to read our Bibles and a brighter light to shine upon its deep and pregnant pages. . . . We need a vivid spiritual concept of what God is saying to us—what His thought in the Word is for each of us."

Be enthusiastic about studying the greatest book ever written! Like the men Jesus met on the road to Emmaus, we should be excited about the Scriptures. Once their eyes were opened they said, "Were not our hearts burning within us while he talked with us on the road and opened the Scriptures to us?"

J. B. Tidwell, a Bible teacher at Baylor University, had some sage advice about studying the Bible. He urged Bible students to "approach God's Word with intelligence, with confidence, with reverence, with a ready assent to its teachings, with purpose to obey it, with a view to self-appropriation, with a spirit of rejoicing in it, with prayerfulness, with a view to finding Jesus in it, and with meditation."

HOW TO STUDY

As you commit to make Bible study a vital part of your Christian experience, there are certain practical decisions you need to make. What method will you use? What type of Bible study will you become involved in? When and where will you study?

Time and Place

Set aside enough time each day for your study. It may be at 4:00 A.M. or 9:00 P.M.—the important thing is to designate a particular time. Be sure to find a time when the telephone and other people will not distract you. Find a comfortable chair, table, or desk to go to each day to study.

Christian author Calvin Miller stresses the importance of not rushing the time we give to God's Word. "We can't dash into his presence and choke down spiritual inwardness before we hurry to our one o'clock appointment," he says. "No one who hurries into the presence of God is content to remain for long."

How to Get Started

Author Henrietta Mears said, "We must come to it with a purpose, with a clearly defined object; we must know what we are about."

Author Kathy Collard Miller suggests that Christians new to intensive Bible study start small. You don't want to feel overwhelmed from the very beginning.

"Don't make big goals. Think small. Instead of thinking that only studying one hour a day will be valuable, start small by making a goal of reading one chapter of the Bible three or four times a week. Then increase the goal little by little," Kathy recommends. "This will be more successful than thinking God is only pleased if I study an hour a day. In reality, He is pleased with any effort we make and will reward us for small steps."

TYPES OF STUDY

We can approach the Bible through several different approaches depending upon our personality, our needs, and how God directs us. We should all be involved in a daily personal Bible study. As Christians who attend a local church, we should all be involved in Sunday School Bible studies where we study and discuss Bible truths. In addition, many churches offer other opportunities for group Bible studies using a variety of works by contemporary authors. Many community Bible studies also exist where people of different denominations come together to study.

Some Christians delve deep into the Bible better alone; others need the fellowship with others in small-group studies such as church Bible study groups or community groups.

Pulpit Study

Listening to the reading and expounding of the Bible by a minister is generally part of most worship services. We need to always be in a reverent attitude when we listen to the reading of the living Word of God. The time we spend in worship services where we study the Word together as a congregation should be a beginning point for the week ahead of personal study.

Personal Study

Designate a time each day for your Bible reading and then decide what book you will study. For example, at the beginning of the year, you might determine to read the entire Bible or to study in depth a major book such as John or the four Gospels (Matthew, Mark, Luke, and John) for the year.

If you have not read the entire Bible, then you might want to read it in order to get an overview of the complete Bible before studying one book in depth.

Another approach is to take one book and immerse yourself in it for a specific period of time. For example, Proverbs has 31 chapters. You might read 1 chapter a day (if the month has 30 days, then read 2 chapters the last day), and you might reread Proverbs in this way for several months. Each month you read the book you will discover new truths.

Some like to study people of the Bible, while others like to delve into themes such as the Holiness of God or the Holy Spirit. Some do key word studies focusing on words such as *grace, salvation, forgiveness,* and *faith.*

Another approach is to study in depth significant chapters or passages such as the Ten Commandments (Ex. 20:1–17), the Sermon on the Mount (Matt. 5:1 to 7:28), or the love chapter (1 Cor. 13).

Richard J. Foster in *Celebration of Discipline* suggests that Christians take personal study one step further: private study retreats. "Some of my most profitable experiences of study," he says, "have come through structuring a private retreat of two to three days' duration."

Sunday School Studies

One of the most meaningful ways Christians can study the Bible in a group setting continues to be through the church Sunday School.

A leader in Christian education through Sunday Schools was Henrietta Mears (1890–1963). She dedicated herself to the Lord at the age of 7. In 1928, she became director of Christian education at First Presbyterian Church in Hollywood, California. There she literally made an impact upon the world.

Sunday School attendance grew under her leadership from 400 to 4,000 within 3 years. She taught in the College Department, where their department's motto was To Know Christ and to Make Him Known, a motto she helped thousands of students make real in their lives. She taught and trained leaders; two of hundreds were Bill Bright who founded Campus Crusade for Christ and Richard Halverson who became chaplain of the US Senate.

Small-Group Studies

Many churches offer opportunities apart from Sunday School for people to be involved in Bible study. Studying the Bible in small-group settings is a wonderful way to share insights with others, develop closer relationships with brothers and sisters in Christ, and delve deeper into the Scriptures.

High school teacher Lisa Howerton recently took part in two small-group Bible studies at her church and found them to be very meaningful. "It was an intergenerational group, which let me see that women of all ages struggle with the same issues," she says. "I learned more about other women in my church and really grew in my faith."

Administrative assistant and grandmother Marilyn Brown has taught many small-group Bible studies over the years. She says that teaching is very much a learning experience in and of itself. "When teaching, to be quite honest, I study right along with the members of the class. I can never know enough; and every time I teach a class, I get as much or more out of it as the members. Every time you read your favorite verse, you get something new from it. That's how it is with teaching Bible study. I am no Bible scholar, but I stay hungry to know more about my Lord," she says.

It's also fulfilling, Marilyn says, to get to know fellow class members better. "The most fulfilling thing about teaching a class is watching the class members grow and learn and hunger to know more," she says. "Each class is different with its own personality and I love seeing it develop."

Community Studies

Margaret Jones, homemaker, mother, and Sunday School teacher, has experienced the power of community Bible studies. More than 25 years ago she attended a local Christian Women's Club luncheon, sponsored by Stonecroft Ministries of Kansas City, Missouri, and was invited to a Friendship Bible Coffee. She remembers the first meeting: "A very good friend and I went to the home where the coffee was held. The ladies were friendly; we had refreshments and visited for a while before the leader got us started. We were given a *Good News Bible* with the study book. All references in the study referred us to a page number in the *Good News Bible* whenever we were to read the Scripture. This made it so easy, and no one was embarrassed if they didn't know the location of the books of the Bible."

Margaret says the study was a turning point in her life. "As I did the lessons and went to the weekly discussions, I began to see the relevance of the Bible to me personally," she says. "I had made a decision many years earlier to trust Jesus Christ as my Savior, but had not seen the Bible as a written guide for my life. I became so excited each week as I discovered the truths of God's Word."

An important part of the study was the revelation of certain Scripture passages. Margaret remembers the day she learned 1 John 1:9 ("If we confess our sins, he is faithful and just and will forgive us our sins and purify us from all unrighteousness"). She says, "How grateful I am for that verse."

Her discovery of Psalm 139:13–16 ("For you created my inmost being; you knit me together in my mother's womb. I praise you because I am fearfully and wonderfully made; your works are wonderful, I know that full well. My frame was not hidden from you when I was made in the secret place. When I was woven together in the depths of the earth, your eyes saw my unformed body. All the days ordained for me were written in your book before one of them came to be") changed the way she looked at herself. "These words lifted me from low self-esteem and showed me my worth to my Creator. God's Word is powerful and to the point. I am so glad that someone invited me to attend that Bible coffee many years ago," Margaret says. "It has been a journey of discovery that never ends."

METHODS OF STUDYING THE BIBLE

In his book, *How to Study the Bible*, Olin Binkley outlines some basic methods for studying the Bible. He cites:

- word study. Understand every English word clearly.
- context. Study the setting or background of the verses you read.
- circumstances of writing. Know who wrote the passages, when they were written, where they were written, and how they were written.
- historical references. Understand the history of the Bible.
- relation to other teachings. Relate verses you read to the rest of the Bible.
- kind of writing. Understand if a passage is poetry, a parable, a prayer, etc.
- leadership of the Spirit. Rely completely on the Holy Spirit for enlightenment.

Kay Arthur incorporates some of the same methods in her many Bible studies. She, and others, call the technique inductive study. "The most important thing you need to remember is that to find out what the Bible says, you need to read it yourself in a way that will help you discover what it says, what it means, and how you are going to apply it to your life," Kay says. This is evidenced in the three parts of Bible study she encourages: observation, interpretation, and application.

She says you must have a willingness to slow down and look at what the Scriptures are truly saying. You do this by first reading them on your own and analyzing what they mean to you; after you have done that, move on to additional helps such as commentaries or written studies.

Reading the Entire Bible

If you "read three chapters a day and five on Sunday, you can read the entire Bible in 362 days," according to Tim LaHaye in *How to Study the*

Bible for Yourself. He tells about the "late Dr. Harry Ironsides [a great Bible teacher] who, at 72 years of age, had read the Bible through for each year of his life." After Ironsides went blind, he continued preaching because he knew most of the Bible by heart.

Hearing such stories, however, can be a bit intimidating. Reading the entire Bible seems to be an impossible task. It's not, however, if you devise a plan for doing so.

Henrietta Mears suggested that one read a book a week. She advised that if you are tackling a longer book such as Genesis, divide it into seven parts so you can complete it in a week. She noted that the Bible can be read (pulpit rate) in approximately 80 hours. We have to schedule that 80 hours, and, of course, longer if we want to study it carefully as we read it.

Bible Study Aids

Many tools—everything from Bible dictionaries, to concordances, to atlases, to online references—can make Bible study much more understandable and accessible. Don't be afraid to use them!

Pastor Joe McKeever says that a good friend of his recommended the *Anchor Bible Dictionary*, and it hasn't disappointed him. "It is mammoth and covers all subjects in great depth. I recommend it highly," he says.

When it comes to concordances, Joe says that any concordance is a valuable concordance. "I have two in my office. *Strong's Concordance* tells you more than you want to know, even listing every use of the word 'the' in the Bible, and an abridged one that is far more usable," he says. "But the concordance I have at home is a gift from a friend at my ordination in 1962 and cost only $2.98. I still use it almost daily."

Kathy Collard Miller cautions that the numbers of study aids can be daunting and suggests that individuals be realistic when they begin using them. "Start using one research book like a dictionary or customs of the Bible or commentary to support your study," she says. "In reading a small passage, just look up the meaning of one word. Again, the idea is start small and then increase."

Bible Study Journal

An excellent practice to supplement your time of Bible study is to keep a journal of your personal Bible study. Tim LaHaye recommends five things to include in a diary:

- God's message to you. Record God's special message to you from your reading.
- A promise from God. Write down a promise from God if it is included in your reading.
- A command to keep. Record in your journal any commands you should obey that come from the Scriptures.
- A timeless principle. Write down divine insights you gain from your reading.
- Personal application. Make practical application from your reading to where you are in your life right now by writing down insights and changes you need to make in your life.

MEMORIZING SCRIPTURE

"How can young people keep their way pure?" the psalmist asked. "By guarding it according to your word. With my whole heart I seek you; do not let me stray from your commandments. I treasure your word in my heart so that I may not sin against you" (Psalm 119:9–11 NRSV).

In past centuries, Christians regularly memorized Scripture. Fanny Crosby, the renowned hymn writer who was blind, could recite the first four books of the Old Testament and the four Gospels by the time she was 10 years old. No wonder she wrote over 8,000 hymns: she knew the Bible.

Frances Havergal, the English writer of such beloved hymns as "Take My Life, and Let It Be Consecrated" and "I Gave My Life for Thee," had a remarkable gift of memory. In addition to knowing six languages, she memorized all of the Gospels and Epistles, as well as Isaiah, the Psalms, the Minor Prophets, and Revelation.

While in a concentration camp during in World War II, Corrie ten Boom said, "There was a time when they took away my Bible. Do you know what they could not take away? All the Scriptures I knew by heart." Romans 8:18 ("I consider that our present sufferings are not worth comparing with the glory that will be revealed in us") and Colossians 1:11 ("Being strengthened with all the power according to his glorious might so that you may have great endurance and patience, and joyfully") helped Corrie survive in the concentration camp.

Abolitionist Sojourner Truth never could read the Bible for herself, but she committed much of the Bible to memory after listening to people read it to her. She frequently quoted the Bible in her speeches.

Although we might not be able to emulate the Frances Havergals or Sojourner Truths of the world, they can inspire us to commit to memory as much Scripture as we can. Each of us will face times in our lives when all we have to call upon is prayer and the Word we have hidden in our hearts.

APPLYING THE BIBLE TO YOUR DAILY LIFE

The Bible is a guide for us, according to the psalmist: "Your word is a lamp to my feet and a light for my path" (Psalm 119:105).

Henrietta Mears said, "Read it seeking for illumination. It is a revelation and He will flash light upon the page as you come humbly."

When reading the Bible each morning, Olympic medalist and missionary Eric Liddell would ask himself this question: "What bearing does this morning's Bible passage have on my life, and what does He want me to do about it?"

As we read the Bible and apply the truths, we will love people more, forgive others, allow God to work in our lives, and use our gifts for His service. God will change our lives when we spend time immersed in His Word.

FAVORITE PASSAGES

According to a recent survey of the Gallup organization, Psalms is the favorite book of the Bible for Americans. Next are Genesis, Matthew, John, Revelation, Proverbs, Job, and Luke.

Missionary Mary Slessor loved the Book of Job. Of Job 28 she wrote, "A very mine of gems and precious things—exquisitely lovely thoughts and language."

Beloved twentieth-century author Eugenia Price had only one bookmark in her Old Testament; it was at her favorite passage: Psalm 139. She loved it because it spoke of God's thoughts about us: "They would outnumber the grains of sand" (Psalm 139:18).

Eugenia thought that the most important verse in the entire Bible was John 1:1 ("In the beginning was the Word, and the Word was with God, and the Word was God") because it "is key to all true understanding of Christianity" and that "the moment in which a human faith grasps the Oneness of God and Jesus, all things become new."

Businesswoman and single mother Cheryl Finch says that her favorite verse has always been Psalm 5:12. "For surely, O Lord, you bless the righteous," it says. "You surround them with your favor as with a shield." She used the verse during her son's and daughter's childhoods, changing it to match each child's name ("O Lord, surround Hunter [or Fletcher] with a shield of righteousness and protect him [her] from the evil one.") The verse has given her much comfort over the last several decades.

"This not only protected them but it gave me peace to know they were in God's care at all times," Cheryl says. "I attribute this prayer to not only protecting my children but also to me because my children have been a delight, joy, and blessing their entire lives."

MEDITATION AND THE BIBLE

Meditation on the Word with the aid of the Holy Spirit helps us apply biblical truths. "Do not let this Book of the Law depart from our mouth; meditate on it day and night, so that you may be careful to do everything written in it" (Josh. 1:8).

Orphanage founder George Mueller said, "Meditation on God's Word has given me the help and strength to pass peacefully through deep trials. . . . Without spiritual preparation, the service, the trials, and the temptations of the day can be overwhelming."

Kay Arthur says that meditation is the key to her times of study in the Bible. "I guard my time and don't neglect my study of the Word of God. I really believe that we need to have leisure time with God. I believe that we are suffering greatly because we do not know God," she says. "I love Joshua 1:7–9, where in essence God tells Joshua that he needs to not just let the Word of God come out of his mouth, but he needs to meditate on it night and day."

PERSONAL QUESTIONS ABOUT BIBLE STUDY

- How much time each week do I devote to personal Bible study?
- Am I consistent in my study of the Bible?
- What steps can I take to make my personal Bible study time more effective and meaningful?
- Am I involved in some type of small-group Bible study?
- Am I reading both the Old Testament and the New Testament?
- Have I ever read the entire Bible? If I haven't, is God leading me to do so?
- Am I allowing the Bible to speak to me daily?
- Am I claiming the promises of the Bible?
- Am I teaching the Bible to my children and grandchildren?

MAKING BIBLE STUDY PART OF YOUR LIFE

- Many translations and types of Bibles exist. Find one that best meets your needs.
- Devote a part of each day to studying the Bible alone without interruption. You might begin with 15 minutes each day for a week, then increase to 30 minutes a day.
- Read through the Bible during the year if you have not.
- Ask God to speak to you through His Word and give you direction.
- As you read the Bible, keep a journal of the spiritual truths that God teaches you.
- Consider participating in small Bible study groups at your church or in community Bible studies.
- Study the Bible with your children and grandchildren.
- Keep your Bible with you near your bed, in your car, in your briefcase, in your purse so it will be available at all times.
- In your Bible study, be alert to verses that will encourage others. Share them verbally or include them in your letters and emails to strengthen both believers and nonbelievers.

• Develop a system that works for you to help you memorize Scripture. For example, copy verses on 3-by-5 cards and put them by your computer, on your mirror, on your refrigerator. Take them with you on your walks; keep them handy while waiting for appointments or in line at the grocery store.
• Commit to memorize one Scripture verse per week.

LIFE APPLICATION VERSE

"For the word of God is living and active. Sharper than any double-edged sword, it penetrates even to dividing soul and spirit, joints and marrow; it judges the thoughts and attitudes of the heart " (Heb. 4:12).

PRAYER

Holy God, thank You for Your Word. Open my heart and mind to understand Your truths and apply them daily to my life. Amen.

3
Worship

"As a true worshiper, your heart will long to worship Him at all times, in all ways and with all of your life"—Darlene Zschech, author of "Shout to the Lord" and other praise songs

"With Jesus' help, let us continually offer our sacrifice of praise to God by proclaiming the glory of His name" (Heb. 13:15 NLT).

Author Liz Curtis Higgs usually attends worship services at her contemporary, 9,300-member church. The services are very familiar and meaningful to her. "We use a mix of contemporary music and updated hymns with a full praise band on Sunday mornings. It is exciting, to say the least!" she says. "That praise time takes up the first 30 minutes of the service and the second half is the sermon."

The best-selling author of *Bad Girls of the Bible*, however, has stepped out of her familiar worship surroundings on numerous occasions. She has found that worship can take place at any time, in all different types of churches and services.

"I visited a friend's church one Ash Wednesday and received ashes on my forehead. That was a new and wonderful experience for me," she remembers. "Another time I attended a conference with 10,000 other believers and we were led through Communion without any elements at all. The pastor simply said, 'Take the bread; take the cup' and we all knew exactly what to do."

Her most meaningful worship experience, though, was when she attended the Moravian church of her childhood. "Not only was I awash in memories, but the music and order of service have been the same for decades upon decades. Some might find that boring or repetitive, but the familiarity of the service allowed me to put aside any concerns about 'What's next?' and simply enter into worship. I cried from first note to last. It was glorious!"

We can worship God in a familiar church, in a cavernous auditorium in an urban church, or in a small white country chapel. We can worship God apart from a special building or an organized service. Worship (whether public, in private, or with family) should move us as Christians beyond the normal concerns of everyday life and elevate us to a closer union with Jesus Christ. In worship, Christians glorify God above and beyond everything else.

The Bible is replete with verses that extol the virtues and importance of worship. David penned hundreds of songs of praise and worship to God; the Book of Psalms is a hymnbook of worship songs. "'Come, let us bow down in worship,'" the psalmist urged. "'Let us kneel before the Lord our Maker'" (Psalm 95:6). Psalm 96:9 says, "Worship the Lord in the splendor of his holiness."

David worshiped God in all circumstances—not just in happiness, but also in sadness, confusion, defeat, and guilt. He teaches us that God is always in control and always worthy of our worship.

Worship, then, should be a priority in our life that we practice in a disciplined manner.

WHAT IS WORSHIP?

Worship is many things to many people.

- It is celebration through singing, thanksgiving, praising, and taking Communion.
- It is fellowship with brothers and sisters in Christ.
- It is education as we listen to teaching and let the Holy Spirit guide us.
- It is meditation as we pray, confess, and consider our relationship with Christ.

Consider what Christians of the past and present tell us about worship:

"Worship is giving God the best that he has given you. Be careful what you do with the best you have. Whenever you get a blessing from God, give it back to Him as a love gift. Take time to meditate before God and offer the blessing back to Him in a deliberate act of worship. . . . God will never let you hold a spiritual thing for yourself, it has to be given back to Him so that He may make it a blessing to others."—*Author Oswald Chambers*

"We must make sure we meet with Him, and that meeting is called 'worship.'"—*Author Jill Briscoe*

"Worship is focusing on and responding to God."—*Author Donald Whitney (Spiritual Disciplines for the Christian Life)*

John Stott says in his book *Christian Basics* that the best biblical definition of worship he knows is to "glory in his holy name" (Psalm 105:3).

Darlene Zschech is worship pastor at Hillsong Church in Sydney, Australia, and the author of such praise songs as "Shout to the Lord," a song that was ranked as one of the ten most popular hymn/worship songs in the October 2001 issue of *Christian Reader*. Darlene believes that worship is not about the songs we sing or the words we pray; it is a matter of the heart and soul.

"True worship is not about the songs, the vocals, the band, or the choir. All of those things contribute towards a great expression of worship, but the essence of worship is when your heart and soul, the core of your being, connects with and adores the Spirit of God," she says.

"Worship is something that is seen by your actions and not just by the words you speak or sing. It isn't a ritual. You don't go to church to go through the motions according to a formula. It involves our heart, mind, and will. Worship is giving yourself completely, in all truth and honesty, that embodies and reflects the selfless generosity of Christ."

Darlene says that we must remember that the word *worship* is a verb. When we worship, we are doing something. "It means to be full of adoration, to bow down, to revere, and to hold in awe the beauty of the Lord," she says.

ROLE OF THE HOLY SPIRIT

Worship is truly meaningful when it involves a partnership between the believer and the Holy Spirit. When that partnership is in place, when we have asked the Holy Spirit to speak to us through our acts of worship, we then experience the sermon, music, prayer, confession, Communion, and fellowship in a new, fresh, and enlightening way.

Poet Pat Taylor says the Holy Spirit speaks to her during worship in a number of ways. He confirms her gifts and gives her guidance. And He helps her understand Scripture in a real way. "The Holy Spirit speaks to me during the service, and I understand exactly what the preacher is saying and know it is not through my own understanding," she says.

TYPES OF WORSHIP

We tend to think of worship as a corporate act, as a public experience with fellow Christians in a church or other house of worship. That, however, is not the only type of worship. There are also family and private worships.

Public Worship

Public worship involves many different elements, all of which vary from church to church. Singing hymns, praying, listening to the pastoral message, taking Communion, confessing, giving, and experiencing fellowship are all substantial parts of the public worship experience.

Ministers speak to millions of people weekly around the world. As the Holy Spirit guides, Christians worship the Lord as they listen and apply the truths of the Scriptures to their lives. As the writer of Hebrews said: "The word of God is living and active. Sharper than any double-edged sword" (Heb. 4:12). God's message through His messengers changes lives.

An integral part of public worship is fellowship with other believers. Missionary Mara Golson learned how important fellowship is to a believer. "I grew up thinking it wasn't a very big deal to miss worship with other people as long as you were still praying and in contact with God," she said. "Then I spent my first year in Russia without access to an English-speaking church. I taught Bible studies and attended one for missionaries in English for a while. The last three months the missionaries quit having the weekly Bible study. Then I went to Greece to stay with friends and get a new Russian visa.

"They took me to their Greek evangelical church. It was nice to be in a building that 'looked like' a church to me—pews, baptistery. They had headphones for me to listen to a translator so I could understand the service. The congregation repeated the Lord's Prayer. Even though they said it in Greek, I took my headphones off and still understood what was being said. I was among a throng of others who believed in the same God I did; we worshiped the same Jesus for the same reasons. I cried so much I couldn't say the words with them. I knew I was among 'family.' Now I understand why Paul spent so much time stressing the unity of the body of Christ. We belong together unlike people who are not members."

Private Worship

We also worship on a personal, private level, creating intimacy with God in a way that few other disciplines can.

Businesswoman Judy Owens has created an intimate private worship center in her home. The area is in her living room and has candles, crosses, and a Bible turned to the story of the disciples meeting Jesus on the road to Emmaus. It also has a picture called *Guardian Angel* she received as a birthday gift from her son and family. It portrays an angel leading children over a bridge.

"The picture is very special to me since it's something I remember seeing at my grandmother's home when I used to visit it in my childhood," she says. The altar also has a poem, "Splinters from the Cross," lying beside it.

All of these items help Judy as she prays and asks for the Holy Spirit's guidance. "I kneel and pray by my worship center. I also lift persons up who are in need of prayer," she explains. "Sometimes I just sit there for quiet time." The center's main purpose, she says, is to serve as "a place to call on the Holy Spirit's intervention in my life."

Family Worship

Families can also experience worship at home. This is an important way to instill a love of worship between married couples and between parents and children.

Amy Nappa, author of such books as *52 Fun Family Devotions* and *52 Fun Family Prayer Adventures*, believes that family worship is of utmost importance today. "The place where children are most likely to learn about God is from the example of their parents. Do the parents model worship? Bible study? Prayer? When children can see their parents doing these things, they realize they are important," Amy says. "And when parents do them with their children, they are teaching their kids how to grow spiritually."

It's important, Amy says, to realize that "children can grow spiritually while they are children." She advises parents to ask themselves what values they are passing on to their children. "What if they've never learned how to grow closer to God? What if they've never learned how to pray?" she asks. "The years when children are at home are wonderful years for parents to guide their children in both growing spiritually and knowing how to continue to grow."

Amy says that worship is an important part of spiritual growth and is something that can be done in the home. "Help children learn how to worship through prayer, song, movement, and other methods. Be creative with it," she says.

COMPONENTS OF WORSHIP

The following components can be part of both private and public worship.

Praise

The psalmist expressed the essence of praising God: "Great is the Lord, and most worthy of praise" (Psalm 48:1).

In his classic book *Morning by Morning*, Charles Spurgeon put praise in its rightful place. "It is not left to our own option whether we shall praise God or not," he wrote. "Praise is God's most righteous due, and every Christian, as the recipient of His grace, is bound to praise God from day to day."

Author Kathy Collard Miller agrees. "Praise is so important. I'm remembering a time I felt so angry at my husband. God told me to praise Him but I didn't want to do it. I finally forced myself to sing a praise chorus and as I did, little by little, my anger dissipated, and I was able to release my unrealistic expectations about my husband's behavior. Praising God made a difference in my human relationships—and strengthens my faith in our wonderful God's attributes."

Praise, then, should be the primary goal of our worship experience. Everything we do in worship should praise and glorify God.

German organist and composer Johann Sebastian Bach (1685–1750) offered his "praise to God" through his musical compositions. A religious spirit marks all of his work. His early years as a church organist and as a court organist prepared him as a composer. From 1723 until his death, he was cantor at St. Thomas's School in Leipzig where he also served as organist. His diverse work included chorale preludes; organ preludes and fugues; concertos; sonatas; and, of course, masses. *The Mass in B Minor* is one of the most significant works of choral literature. His work revolved around the Lutheran church year including masses and cantatas such as the *Christmas Oratorio*.

At the end of his religious work appears *Soli Deo Gloria* (To God Alone the Glory). In his secular music he would often write at the head the letters INJ (*In Nomine Jesu*). Every note he wrote celebrated the glory of God. This spirit is the source of the joy that is so apparent in his work. Today his work permeates the hearts and minds of musicians and listeners everywhere. His music continues to bring joy to people of faith.

Thanksgiving

The Bible says much about our giving thanks to God. The psalmist said, "Enter his gates with thanksgiving and his courts with praise; give thanks to him and praise his name" (Psalm 100:4). And again in Psalm 138:1 (NRSV) we find, "I give you thanks, O Lord, with my whole heart."

Adoration

We are to worship in adoration of God. As David put it so well in Psalm 145:1–3: "I will exalt you, my God the King; I will praise your name for ever and ever. Every day I will praise you and extol your name for ever and ever. Great is the Lord and most worthy of praise; his greatness no one can fathom."

Prayer

Prayer is an integral part of any worship experience. We offer our acts of worship to God in prayer; we pray for guidance; we pray in thankfulness; we pray in confession. Worship could truly not exist apart from prayer!

Bill Hybels, the founder/pastor of Chicago's Willow Creek Community Church, says that we need only look to the New Testament to see the importance of prayer in worship.

"The New Testament tells us that the early Christians devoted themselves to prayer," he says. "When we read about the early church we discover that prayer was in the center of their personal lives and in the heart of their life as a community."

Confession

Confession is a vital part of the worship experience. We cannot truly experience worship to its fullest unless we are right with God, unless we have confessed our sins to others and to Him first.

Confession, in the forum of worship, evidences itself as either corporate confession through prayers of confession or in the form of private, individual confession. It also comes in the form of public confession of Jesus Christ as Savior and through baptism.

Pat Taylor will always fondly remember one worship experience in particular, the one in which her two sons publicly confessed their faith in Christ. "Eleven months after Jeff made this confession and was saved, he had a motorcycle wreck and was brain damaged," she says. "Two and a half years later he passed away. So that worship service is the most special to me. It reminds me that I will see him again one day."

Communion

Jesus instituted the Lord's Supper and instructed His disciples to celebrate it regularly. When we partake of Communion, we need to comprehend its spiritual importance, remembering Christ's amazing sacrifice for us. When the words are spoken ("This is His blood"; "This is His body"), we need to recognize the importance of His act on a personal level.

Bill Hybels compares Communion to an experience he had soon after his father's death. In digging through some boxes during a move, Bill's wife uncovered a photograph of Bill and his father standing in front of his airplane. The picture was taken two weeks before his father died. Bill says that at that moment the floodgates of emotion opened and he remembered his father's significance in his life. The photograph became a tangible reminder of who his father had been.

"That is the very reason God has given us Communion," Bill says. "This is why we take the bread and the cup. They remind us of the One Who loves us beyond description. These moments open the floodgates and help us reminisce about what Jesus means to us."

Singing

Few of us can imagine a worship experience without singing. The Bible says we are to "sing joyfully to the Lord, you righteous" (Psalm 33:1) and offers us many examples of how singing is connected to worship.

David chose singing and music as his primary avenue of worship; the Psalms are full of commands to "sing unto the Lord." The psalmist proclaimed, "Come, let us sing for joy to the Lord; let us shout aloud to the Rock of our salvation. Let us come before him with thanksgiving and extol him with music and song" (Psalm 95:1).

When Paul and Silas found themselves thrown into prison for preaching the gospel, they worshiped God through singing. As Luke recorded, "About midnight, Paul and Silas were praying and singing hymns to God, and the other prisoners were listening" (Acts 16:25).

Darlene Zschech says we must never feel inadequate because we are not singers of professional caliber. God wants our "joyful noise" even if that's all it is—noise. "The Scripture tells you to bring an offering, even if you feel like you have nothing to bring. All God wants is your heart," she says. "He doesn't need your talent, your musical ability, or all the things you can do. He wants you!"

"You don't have to be the greatest singer or musician to be a great worshiper," she continues. "Whether you are in the body, or as an individual, open your heart and adore the Lord from the very core of your being. That's all He's asking."

Playing an instrument

For almost 35 years financial analyst Jim Bagby has experienced worship while he plays the piano for church services, prayer services, community services, weddings, funerals, and his church choir. "From the first choir rehearsal on that first day, I knew this was the place God desired to use me, if I would only let Him," he says. "As long as I obeyed Him by playing directly 'unto Him,' He would give me the courage to play before any number of people which happen to assemble for the purpose of worshiping Him."

Jim says that his personal worship experience becomes extremely powerful when he's playing the piano. "When I play for church, I feel a mighty 'covering,' even to the point where my skin 'tingles,' of the great power and love of our Lord Jesus Christ. Playing is indeed my way of praising and entering into the presence of my Savior," he explains.

Playing during Communion is also a worshipful experience for him. "Many times there is no singing during Communion, only the sound of my pastor discussing the sacred Blood and Body of our Lord accompanied by the soft background praise music of the piano," he says. "During these times, I feel particularly close to God, bathed in His precious presence and love."

He also plays during altar calls and times of invitation. "I feel God uses my music to create an atmosphere of worship and praise where people feel perhaps a bit more freed and persuaded to give their all to the Lord," he says.

Dancing

Following the safe passage of the Israelites through the Red Sea and past the armies of the Egyptians, Miriam led the people in a special time of worship. The Bible says, "Then Miriam the prophetess, Aaron's sister, took a tambourine in her hand, and all the women followed her, with tambourines and dancing. Miriam sang to them: 'Sing to the Lord, for he is highly exalted. The horse and its rider he has hurled into the sea'" (Ex. 15:20).

As King David supervised the return of the ark of the covenant to Jerusalem, his people played loud music and shouted joyfully. The king's own behavior, however, was even more noticeable. In 2 Samuel

6:14 we read, "David . . . danced before the Lord with all his might."

Dance often found a place in worship throughout the Bible, and it continues to do so today in many worship experiences. College student Melissa Levins, who began ballet lessons at the age of 4, uses her dancing talent as a way to express her love for Christ. "When I'm dancing to a worship song, I get the sense that I'm not dancing for anyone but God. It is a very peaceful and energetic feeling," she says. "But dancing for God is not true worship unless the movements and the choreography come straight from your heart, just like any other form of worship."

PREPARING FOR WORSHIP

To have a deep, meaningful worship experience, we must prepare for it. We must align our minds and hearts with God's and anticipate the worship experience with expectation and hope.

Ryan Goodman says that he prepares for worship services by listening to the right kind of music. "I try to listen to as much Christian music as possible, but especially in preparing for worship," he says. "I also like some alone time for prayer and meditation."

Pat Taylor uses a similar tactic. "If I am on my way to church, I listen to a gospel tape of singing; and by the time I get there, I am in a happy mood, my troubles seem far away, and I am ready to worship," she says. "I also prepare for worship by asking God to forgive me and cleanse my heart from all the worldly things around me."

WORSHIP AS A WAY OF LIFE

Worship is not something that takes place just once or twice a week. It should be a daily, hourly, continual experience with God.

Worship changes us. As our 30th President Calvin Coolidge (1872–1933) so aptly said, "It is only when men begin to worship that they begin to grow."

"Therefore, I urge you, . . . in view of God's mercy, to offer your bodies as living sacrifices, holy and pleasing to God—this is your spiritual act of worship," wrote Paul to the Romans (Rom. 12:1). We worship God when we continually offer ourselves as living sacrifices.

Worship prepares us to use our gifts for God's service. Paul speaks of using our gifts in the verses that follow in Romans 12:3–13.

Hymn writer Fanny Crosby (1820–1915) led a life of worship and used her gifts to glorify God and others. She was the most prolific writer of gospel songs in American history. Her blindness at six weeks of age didn't keep her from composing, being a friend to several US presidents, speaking before the US Senate (the first woman to do so), and doing missions and evangelistic work.

Her hymns—including "Blessed Assurance"; "To God Be the Glory"; "Rescue the Perishing"; and "Pass Me Not, O Gentle Savior" (a favorite of Queen Victoria's)—touched countless lives and continue to do so today. Her goal was to bring salvation to people through her songs. For most of her life she lived among the poor. At the age of 60 she began missions work in New York City's Bowery, one of America's most depressing places. She brought love to alcoholics, prostitutes, and derelicts. Considering missions work her main occupation for many years, she wrote hymns urging people to make decisions for Christ.

Matt Donnelly, an editor for ChristianityToday.com, says that worship is something to be contemplated in each moment of our lives.

"Often we go to church on Sunday to worship. There we pray and reflect and come away with a sense of God's presence in our lives. Then what? What about the other six days in the week? How do we worship God when we're changing diapers, negotiating a contract, or taking the kids to soccer practice?

"We can worship in those situations by seeking to do everything for the glory of God. In other words, we worship God when we allow our thoughts and actions to be used to reveal Who Jesus is. We might not be able to share the gospel in every situation, but we can at least attempt to manifest the fruit of the Spirit and try to love our neighbor as ourselves.

"If we see our whole lives as filled with opportunities to worship God, then we'll have a new sense of purpose. No longer will we think worship is only on Sunday or when we're having our quiet time. Worship will become an active thing, an integral part of our everyday lives in the world.

"Because God is Spirit, our worship of him cannot be confined to a building. It must spill over into the entire world, impacting the lives of those around us with the life-changing message of God's love."

PERSONAL QUESTIONS ABOUT WORSHIP

• What is my view of worship? Do I view it as a Sunday-only activity?
• How can I prepare better for my public worship experiences?
• How can I worship God through the use of my gifts?
• Will I consider making time for private worship in my home?
• What aspect of worship is most meaningful to me?
• Do I believe my life is to be an act of worship? If so, how does my daily lifestyle reflect this?

MAKING WORSHIP MORE MEANINGFUL IN YOUR LIFE

• Read prayers of worship in the Bible such as David's in 1 Chronicles 29:11.
• Read the Book of Psalms. Many of them are praise hymns such as Psalms 34, 96, 103, 111, 146, and 147.
• Use a hymnbook and sing/meditate on some of the great songs of worship/praise: "Holy, Holy, Holy"; "Because He Lives"; and "How Great Thou Art." These songs will fix your attention on God.
• Read stories about how the great hymns of worship were written. The stories will inspire you and make the songs more meaningful to you.
• When you feel anxious or worried, try worshiping the Lord in praise and song.
• When you see a rainbow, a flower in bloom, a sunset, worship God the Creator.
• Pause during the day to worship God while driving, gardening, or washing dishes.
• Sing praise songs with your children such as "Praise Him, All Ye Little Children."
• Before falling asleep at night, repeat a Bible verse, a praise song, or a favorite hymn.

LIFE APPLICATION VERSE

"Praise the Lord. Praise the Lord, O my soul. I will praise the Lord all my life: I will sing praise to my God as long as I live" (Psalm 146:1–2).

PRAYER

God, help me to worship You in my prayertime, my Bible study, my times of solitude, my giving, my service, my daily activities—with my life. Amen.

4
Personal Witnessing

"We are all missionaries. . . . Wherever we go, we either bring people nearer to Christ, or we repel them from Christ."—Eric Liddell (1902–1945), Olympic medal winner and missionary to China

"Conduct yourselves in a manner worthy of the gospel of Christ" (Phil. 1:27).

Vonette Bright, the cofounder of Campus Crusade for Christ and host of the radio show *Women Today*, tells the story of a friend who looks for witnessing opportunities in all places and at all times. One of his encounters occurred on an airplane.

Her friend, Glenn Jones, noticed the perfume his flight attendant wore and considered that his wife would probably like the scent. He asked the young woman what she was wearing. She answered, "It's Eternity, by Calvin Klein."

"Glenn, who was so attuned to God, saw this as an opportunity to introduce the gospel," Vonette says. "He asked the attendant, 'Have you heard about eternity by Jesus Christ?' In the moments that followed, Glenn shared the gospel message with her. And she trusted Jesus Christ."

Vonette says that story reminded her that we, as Christians, have eternity at our fingertips—and it's not found in a bottle. It is our responsibility and privilege to share that saving knowledge with others.

Christ calls us to be His witnesses. The Bible teaches us to tell others what we know. Jesus said, "'You will receive power when the Holy Spirit comes on you; and you will be my witnesses in Jerusalem, and in all Judea and Samaria, and to the ends of the earth'" (Acts 1:8).

The great evangelist Billy Graham says that he looks at every situation as an opportunity to share his faith with others. "I never go to see important people, or anyone else, without having the deep realization that I am—first and foremost—an ambassador of the King of kings and Lord of lords. From the moment I enter the room, I am thinking about how I can get the conversation around to the gospel," he says. "We may discuss a dozen peripheral things first, but I am always thinking of ways I can share Christ and His message of hope with them."

Personal witnessing, then, is a spiritual discipline we must cultivate as much as we nurture Bible study, prayer, or worship. We must learn, like Billy Graham and Glenn and Vonette have, to look for ways in our daily lives to share the good news of Christ with everyone around us.

WHY WITNESS?

What was the first thing you did after becoming engaged to be married? Finding out you were pregnant? Getting that long-awaited job?

You probably told someone.

Our salvation in Christ is so much more important! How could we not want to share this incredible news with others?

It is natural and necessary for a Christian to share his or her faith. Our salvation and the peace and joy we have are good news. Out of our gratitude to God, we should declare through our words, actions, and lifestyle what God has done for us.

As the great colonial theologian Jonathan Edwards (1703–1758) said, "The gospel has seemed to me the richest treasure; the treasure that I have most desired, and longed that it might dwell richly in me. The way of salvation by Christ, has appeared, in a general way, glorious and excellent, most pleasant and most beautiful."

We witness not only because it is a natural extension of our faith in Christ but because Christ Himself set an example for us.

Jesus: The Good News

The greatest mission of Christ was to bring others to Him and to His Father. As His followers we reach out to others with our story of grace and salvation.

The New Testament contains numerous stories of Jesus telling others the good news of salvation. He told Nicodemus that "no one can see the kingdom of God unless he is born again" (John 3:3). He gave the Samaritan woman the good news that "whoever drinks the water I give him will never thirst" (John 4:14). He reached out to Zacchaeus and his family, telling him that "the Son of Man came to seek and to save what was lost" (Luke 19:10). He continued to share the salvation story at His crucifixion as He ministered to the thief on the cross next to Him telling him, "'Today, you will be with me in Paradise'" (Luke 23:43).

Jesus instructed His disciples to be soul winners. "Follow me," He said, "and I will make you fish for people" (Matt. 4:19 NRSV).

All four Gospels end with the admonition of Jesus to be witnesses. The Great Commission states, "'Therefore go and make disciples of all nations, baptizing them in the name of the Father and of the Son and of the Holy Spirit'" (Matt. 28:19).

The great nineteenth-century evangelist Dwight L. Moody (1837–1899) took the words of Jesus seriously. He traveled more than a million miles, addressed more than 100 million people, and prayed personally with 750,000 men and women. In America, Great Britain, and Canada he preached a simple, direct message with conviction and power. A contemporary said of him, "The gospel was to him the power of God, and as he talked about it we knew that he had seen it work again and again, and to us it became something not to be talked about, but to be tried and passed on."

Jesus: The Only Way

Like D. L. Moody, we should witness because we know that Jesus is the only way to salvation. "'I am the way and the truth and the life,'" Jesus said. "'No one comes to the father except through me'" (John 14:6).

That most familiar verse of all, John 3:16 (NASB), puts it most succinctly, "For God so loved the world that He gave His only begotten Son, that whoever believes in Him should not perish, but have eternal life."

Paul wrote to the Ephesians, "For it is by grace you have been saved, through faith—and this not from yourselves, it is the gift of God—not by works, so that no one can boast" (Eph. 2:8).

Only Jesus can meet our deepest needs. "'I am the resurrection and the life. He who believes in me will live, even though he dies; and whoever lives and believes in me will never die. Do you believe this?'" (John 11:25–26).

When we understand this need for forgiveness that only Christ can give and then experience a personal relationship with this Christ, we have an insatiable desire for the rest of the world to experience the same thing. We want our friends, family members, extended relatives, co-workers, even strangers on the street to know this forgiveness and to have this relationship.

A story from the life of Helen Keller illustrates this longing for God. After Helen's teacher Anne Sullivan learned to communicate with Helen, she wanted to tell her about God. Helen's spirit rose as she said, "I know Him! I know Him! I didn't know His name."

Do you know Christ personally? Do you want others to know Him in the same way?

DESIRE TO WITNESS

Anne Graham Lotz, daughter of Billy and Ruth Graham, a successful evangelist, and founder of AnGeL Ministries, says that she didn't always have the personal desire to witness. That changed one day with her husband at an evangelism conference in Switzerland.

"As we mingled with evangelical leaders from all over the world who were exploring ways to take the gospel to the ends of the earth, I was ashamed to admit I had never taken it to my next-door neighbors," she remembers.

She went home renewed and dedicated to personal evangelism. "I acted quickly before I lost my nerve," she says. "I invited a dozen neighbors to my home for coffee with the intention of telling them about Jesus Christ. Only four showed up!"

She awkwardly shared her testimony with the four women (so ineptly, she says, that today they don't remember what she actually told them!), but it was an important moment in her life.

"It was a watershed experience for me," she says. "I had crossed over the line."

As Christians we should love others and long for their salvation. We should also look at our neighbors and realize they too need Jesus.

Like Paul we must have a passion for the unsaved. He described his concern for others as "great sorrow and unceasing anguish in my heart" (Rom. 9:2).

William Carey (1761–1834) shared Paul's passion. In a small cottage in Moulton, England, in the 1780s the young man who had already mastered six languages covered his walls with hand-drawn maps of the world. On the different countries he wrote their population, climate, vegetation, animals, and religion. It has been said that "he had a fuller account on his wall maps of the state of the whole world than anyone else living of whom we have record."

William Carey was "mapping" out a biblical perspective to take the gospel to the entire world, a revolutionary thought for his day.

In 1792 he published *An Enquiry into the Obligations of Christians to Use Means for the Conversion of the Heathens*, in which he stated that it was the *duty* of Christians to evangelize. That same year he preached at a Baptist meeting his now famous sermon on Isaiah 54:2. His words "Attempt great things [for God]; Expect great things [from God]" stirred participants to establish a foreign missions organization, the Particular Baptist Society for the Propagation of the Gospel. Thus began the modern missionary movement.

Carey reached India in 1793 where he labored tirelessly for over 40 years. His prodigious output is mind-boggling to all who study his life and example. He helped translate the Scriptures into 44 languages; founded 26 churches and 126 schools; organized India's first medical mission, savings bank, seminary, and Indian girls school newspaper. His efforts led to the first printing operation, paper mill, and steam engine. He worked vigorously for many years for the eradication of suttee (burning widows on their husbands' funeral pyres). Finally, in 1829 his efforts succeeded when suttee was declared a homicide.

WHY DON'T WE WITNESS?

If we have such wonderful news, why don't we share it with others? What holds us back?

Esther Burroughs, a contemporary author and women's ministry speaker, says that the fear factor keeps many Christians from being effective witnesses. "We think that if we share Christ, the person could reject us and what we say," she says. "The whole point is we are talking to them about Jesus Christ; and if they reject our witness, they are rejecting Christ, not us.

"Women are also afraid that they will not have the correct answer or know enough about the Bible. The only correct answer is to tell your own story about your personal relationship with Christ. Your story is authentic. It happened to you.

"Christians get bold about sharing the gospel when fear is taken out of evangelism," Esther says. "When they see that the gospel can be shared in a simple way using their own testimony, tracts, or Bible verses, they are no longer fearful."

Esther stresses that the best way to overcome fear in witnessing is to realize that there is no wrong answer. Simply share your personal experiences with others. "Being a witness is not about memorized presentation," she says. "It is simply talking about the Lord and His reality in your everyday living."

English Baptist minister Charles Spurgeon, who spoke to audiences of 10,000, put witnessing into perspective perfectly. "Holy boldness honors the gospel. . . . To preach the gospel boldly is to deliver it as such a message ought to be delivered. Blush to preach of a dying Savior? Apologize for talking about the Son of God condescending to be made man, that he might redeem us from all iniquity? *Never!* Oh, by the grace of God let us purpose with Paul 'to be yet more bold,' that the gospel may be yet more fully preached throughout all ranks of mankind."

WITNESSING=DISCIPLINE AND PREPARATION

Discipline and preparation are two vital keys to success as an effective witness. We must be disciplined in our actions and prepared with a plan to reach others.

Do you only associate with Christians? Are most of your friends fellow church members? Make it a priority, then, to make some new friends! Look at your neighborhood, workplace, and the places you visit often.

Be open to opportunities to reach out and share your faith. The key to being an effective, comfortable witness is to see every encounter and interruption as an opportunity to reach others. "Live daily to expect an interruption as a divine appointment from God," Esther advises.

Be involved in Bible study and prayer. Cover all of your witnessing efforts in prayer; ask the Holy Spirit to guide you as you go. Study the Bible for encouragement and instruction; know Bible verses to share and give examples from the Bible when appropriate.

Esther says that she uses her quiet time as an opportunity to prepare for witnessing. "We never witness on our own ability, we do so only from the overflow of our walk with God," she says. "During Bible study, the Spirit is teaching and feeding us. I pray daily, thanking God for another day, asking to be clothed in the power of the Holy Spirit and make me obedient."

What can we pray for? Pray for guidance, wisdom, and boldness. Pray that God will lead you to the right people.

Get some training. If you feel inadequate, search for ways to feel empowered. Read books on witnessing techniques, enroll in a training course, develop a mentor relationship with a Christian you see as a powerful witness.

Develop your own testimony. Karla Worley, an author and Dove Award–winning singer/songwriter, has participated in a number of missions trips. She has learned to prepare what she calls her one-minute testimony. "You never know when the opportunity may arise or your leader may point to you and say that it's your turn to tell your story," Karla says. "Everybody's story is different because everybody's story is personal."

Karla says that your testimony is simple: (1) what your life was like before Christ; (2) how you came to know and believe in Jesus; and (3) what difference Jesus has made in your life.

Have the right attitude. In preparing to be a better witness in your daily life, always be respectful and supportive of the other person; communicate friendship, love, sincerity, tactfulness, calmness, and honesty. Listen to the person; establish a rapport; don't argue.

Keep it simple. Francis Schaeffer (1912–1984), who with his wife, Edith, founded L'Abri Fellowship in Switzerland as a study center for thoughtful believers and seekers, had a favorite hymn: "Jesus Loves Me." One of the most eminent Christian scholars of the twentieth century, Francis Schaeffer discovered as he talked with people who needed intellectual answers to their questions that they also needed a direct message to their hearts. He found that "Jesus loves me; this I know" explained the gospel in a clear simple way that led to peace.

If we obediently go where God leads, the Holy Spirit will do the rest. We are to plant the seed; the Holy Spirit will convict and guide.

The Holy Spirit will also encourage us by giving us the right words and the right opportunities. Jesus said in John 14:26, "'The Holy Spirit . . . will teach you all things and will remind you of everything I have said to you.'"

God is already at work in the lives of those who need Him. We are His instruments to help lead people to Him. "The moment we receive Christ as our Savior we also receive the gift of the Holy Spirit. He is the person Who will help us live like and for Christ," Esther says. "The empowering of the Holy Spirit is a continual process. As the Spirit empowers, we live under His control."

HOW DO I WITNESS?

Realize that God uses different methods, people, and techniques to draw people to Him. Our arsenal for personal witnessing, then, is large and varied. Some people are comfortable passing out tracts, while others feel more called to pray for the unsaved.

Remember that Jesus dealt with each person He met on an individual basis and based on that person's life experience. For example, He approached Nicodemus and the Samaritan woman from their backgrounds. We should do the same when we witness. Intellectuals have to be approached in different ways than the uneducated, the community leader from the town drunk.

Some ways to witness include:

Pray

Every Christian can pray for the unsaved. Countless children have been converted because of the prayers of their parents; parents have been converted because of the prayers of their children. Behind every great evangelist and every great minister of the gospel have been faithful pray-ers lifting them up to God.

J. Hudson Taylor (1832–1905), founder of the China Inland Mission, learned about the power of prayer from his mother. One day when he was 17 he was home alone reading a religious leaflet in his father's library. He later said he was reading "in an utterly unconcerned state of mind." His mother was 70 miles away in a room alone praying for his conversion. She prayed hour after hour until until she "was constrained to praise God for that which His Spirit taught her had already been accomplished—the conversion of her son."

While she was praying, Hudson was reading the tract and was impressed with the phrase, "the finished work of Christ." He thought, "If the whole work was finished and the whole debt paid, what is there left for me to do?" He then fell on his knees and accepted Christ. When his mother returned home, he told her he had good news. She said, "I know, my boy, I have been rejoicing in the glad tidings you have to tell me."

Share the Bible

Would you be surprised to know that not everyone owns a Bible? Giving away a Bible could change someone's life! You can also share Bible verses. Some that communicate the plan of salvation are John 3:16; Revelation 3:20; Romans 3:23; 6:23; Acts 8:37; Romans 10:8–12; John 1:12; and Acts 16:30.

As you share the Bible with someone, use it reverently but also naturally. It's been proven that an unbeliever responds better to the Bible when it is read rather than quoted.

Tell your personal faith story

You don't have to be on an evangelism or visitation team from your church to tell your personal faith story. Most effective witnessing comes through building relationships: speaking about the gospel on the job, talking with your friends over a backyard cookout, speaking about Christ while shopping at the mall, telling about the joy you have in Christ at the gym.

Share your relationship with the Lord and how He is important to your life. Tell how He has helped you in specific ways during your life.

Invite people to hear the gospel

Sometimes an invitation is all a person is waiting for, so invite a friend, neighbor, family member, or acquaintance to church, revival meetings, women's meeting, Bible study, Vacation Bible School, potluck meal, or choir presentation. George Barna, a statistician who studies Christian issues, believes that 40 percent of people would come to church if invited.

Many people throughout history have been converted at preaching or revival services. The great evangelists of the past (John Wesley, George Whitefield, Dwight Moody) reached millions for Christ. It has been estimated that John Wesley preached 40,000 times in his life and traveled over 250,000 miles on land as an itinerant minister. Between 1736 and 1770, English evangelist George Whitefield (1714–1770) preached more than 18,000 sermons. He made seven trips to the colonies. It is probable that as many as 80 percent of those living in America during this time actually heard Whitefield speak at least once.

In this century, evangelists Billy Graham and his son Franklin are at the forefront of the many that are still carrying out the message that Wesley, Whitefield, and Moody so tirelessly expounded.

Use a particular witnessing plan

A number of tools and plans can help you become a more effective witness. You can use a gospel presentation tract and/or Scripture portion or follow the ABC's of salvation, the FAITH acrostic, or the Roman Road.

The ABC outline is:

- *Admit* to God that you are a sinner and then repent (Rom. 3:23; 3:10–18).
- *Believe.* By faith receive Jesus Christ as God's Son and accept Jesus' gift of forgiveness (John 3:16).

- *Confess* your faith in Christ as Savior and Lord (Rom. 10:9–10).

FAITH involves sharing the following:

- F *is for forgiveness.* We must have God's forgiveness for our sins. "In him [Jesus] we have redemption through his blood, the forgiveness of sins" (Eph. 1:7).
- A *is for available.* Forgiveness is available for all. "'For God so loved the world that he gave his one and only son, that whoever believes in him shall not perish but have eternal life'" (John 3:16).
- I *is for impossible.* It is impossible for God to allow sin into heaven. "For all have sinned and fall short of the glory of God" (Rom. 3:23).
- T *is for turn.* Turn means *repent,* turn away from sin. "If you confess with your mouth, 'Jesus is Lord,' and believe in your heart that God raised Him from the dead, you will be saved" (Rom. 10:9).
- H *is for heaven.* Heaven is eternal life. "And if I go and prepare a place for you, I will come back and take you to be with me that you also may be where I am" (John 14:3).

The Roman Road is also a plan to follow in leading someone through the plan of salvation:

- "For all have sinned and fall short of the glory of God" (Rom. 3:23).
- "But God demonstrates His own love for us in this: While we were still sinners, Christ died for us" (Rom. 5:8).
- "The wages of sin is death, but the gift of God is eternal life" (Rom. 6:23).
- "If you confess with your mouth, 'Jesus is Lord,' and believe in your heart that God raised him from the dead, you will be saved. For it is with your heart that you believe and are justified, and it is with your mouth that you confess and are saved" (Rom. 10: 9–10).

Esther Burroughs was able to use this method on a recent business trip to Richmond, Virginia. The hotel maid entered the room and, when Esther asked how she was, she defeatedly said that someone had stolen $60 from her and she now had no money to pay her rent.

After learning that the maid hadn't attended church since her childhood, Esther asked her, "Has anyone ever told you about Jesus?"

"No one has ever told me about Him," she answered. "Can He help? Can you tell me about Him?"

They sat down together, and Esther led her through the verses in Romans. "She quietly prayed a prayer to invite Christ into her heart," Esther remembers. While the maid cleaned her bathroom, Esther put $60, a note, and a tract in an envelope for her. She asked her not to open it until that evening.

Soon after the maid left, Esther heard a knock on her door. "I came back to tell you something," the maid said, standing there. "I feel so clean all over. And when you read to me from that book, I felt something coming from you to me."

Esther explained that that's what happens when Christ and the Holy Spirit come into our lives.

Share books

Has a book ever had a major impact on your life? If so, consider sharing it with an unsaved friend. It's a wonderful way to witness to others.

Charles Colson, a former Watergate co-conspirator and now the founder of Prison Ministries International, was converted when a friend gave him C. S. Lewis's *Mere Christianity* to read.

Sammie Barstow, a judicial assistant and mother of two grown daughters, was converted after reading a Christian novel. When she was 9, Sammie began to have a sense of what becoming a Christian involves. Adult leaders gently mentored her toward a decision for Christ, but she wasn't quite ready.

While living in Virginia, she went to the library every Saturday, checked out seven books, and read a book a day throughout the week. "Back then there were few Christian fiction writers," Sammie says, "but I found Grace Livingston Hill and read all her books. One Sunday afternoon, sitting at our kitchen table, reading one of her books, I realized that I needed Christ in my life. So I made that decision right then and asked Him to be my Savior. Although in my early adulthood I spent a number of years out of fellowship with the Lord, I have never doubted the sincerity of my salvation that Sunday afternoon."

Write letters and/or send emails

After his conversion, John Newton (1725–1807) was encouraged to witness to what the Lord had done for him. He insisted that he was not a good speaker but said, "I am a great letter writer and in this way do much witnessing." Newton went on to become a pastor in England for 43 years. His testimony, *An Authentic Narrative*, in the form of 14 letters addressed to a minister friend was published in 1764 and later in nine editions. Although he wrote 280 hymns, John Newton's witness to God's power is most famous in his great hymn "Amazing Grace."

Before his death John told a friend at his bedside, "My memory is nearly gone, but I remember two things: That I am a great sinner and that Christ is a great Savior." He wrote his own epitaph which includes the following: "Once an infidel and libertine, a servant of slaves in Africa, was, by the rich mercy of our Lord and Savior, Jesus Christ preserved, restored, pardoned, and appointed to preach the faith he had long labored to destroy." What a fitting testament and witness!

Letters and emails can still have that same power today. Consider writing a letter to someone who needs to receive a word about Christ from you; forward emails to unsaved friends that testify to God's grace.

Stay-at-home mother Misty Walker has been witnessing for years to her grandmother through letters. Because of strained family relationships, Misty's grandmother didn't know Misty existed until she was 15. Misty decided then it was time to write her. "I've written for the last 11 years, and she never responded until recently," Misty says. "All those years, I kept writing and I told her that God had put her on my heart, and I was going to keep writing her. I would tell her that God loved her and that she would find I was consistent in loving her and praying for her because of the power of God. I told her that in myself I was sinful and selfish and proud and haughty, and only through the love of God was I anything."

Misty and her family were finally invited to Phoenix to meet her grandmother recently. "We stayed at a hotel, but went out to eat; and Tom trimmed her trees and did some minor repair work around her house," Misty says. "She tried to pay him and he turned her down, saying that it was the love of God in him. He was doing it because he was a Christian and it was his way to show her God's love."

Misty's grandmother has not accepted Christ, but Misty stays diligent in her letter writing and her praying.

Use hymns

Many great hymns of the faith have been instrumental in bringing people to God. One that has had tremendous impact is Charlotte Elliott's "Just As I Am." Evangelist D. L. Moody said that the hymn drew as many people to the Lord as his preaching did. Billy Graham's conversion took place during a church service; he went to the altar while "Just As I Am" was sung. Consequently, in his crusades he uses the hymn as a call to commitment.

Evelyn Bence in *Spiritual Moments with the Great Hymns* tells the story of her friend Peggy who came to Christ through a movie and a hymn. Peggy watched the 1985 movie *The Trip to Bountiful* which told the story of an older woman's obsession to get back to her homestead in Bountiful, Texas. Peggy said, "I turned on the TV and there were two women riding on a bus, talking. . . . Then came the song: 'Softly and tenderly Jesus is calling.' The image flashed into my mind of Jesus standing on a rock beckoning me with soft and loving eyes." For weeks Peggy said, "I sang that song and tried to learn the words." She said that she sang and cried while doing her housework. One day Peggy said her husband started singing the song. When she asked him how he knew the song, he said it was an old hymn. Peggy said she felt the song was "a personal call from Jesus to me to open my heart to him."

Show Christian movies

The *Jesus* film, which is distributed through the Campus Crusade for Christ organization, has reached unbelievers around the world with the gospel.

When it was shown in a rural village in China, exciting results took place. A team of Christian workers visited a previously unevangelized remote village to share the gospel. After viewing the *Jesus* film, the villagers told their guests they wanted two months to think things over. The workers left, but gave some evangelistic materials to the villagers.

Two months later when the Christians returned, they were warmly greeted. They realized that God had been working in the village. The villagers had been listening to the taped version of the *Jesus* film. One of the young men of the village had traveled outside the village and returned to tell them that there was something better to be found in life than what they had always known. Thus, on the night the Christians returned to the village, the entire village of 50 people prayed to receive Christ as their Savior!

Live a godly life

In a world in which many people don't attend church, don't own a Bible, and have no real spiritual foundation, perhaps the greatest way we can witness is through our lifestyles, often called lifestyle evangelism.

To be this kind of example, we have to maintain a close relationship with Christ by praying regularly, reading our Bible, having regular fellowship with other Christians through church, and serving Christ sacrificially. Then, once people see the way we live, we must tell them about our Savior.

Corrie ten Boom (1892–1983) said, "If people don't see Jesus in the Bible, this is not your fault. But if they don't see Him in your life, that is your fault." She had a great love for others. "The Gospel is not a secret to be hoarded," she once said, "but a story to be heralded."

She certainly was a herald of the gospel.

The story of Corrie ten Boom is familiar to many Christians because of her best-selling autobiography and film based on the book *The Hiding Place*. She was an ordinary woman of 52 when the Nazis occupied her town of Haarlem in the Netherlands. She and her family opened their home as a "hiding place" for Jews seeking refuge. Betrayed and arrested, her family was imprisoned in February 1944.

Corrie and her sister, Betsie, were sent to the infamous Ravensbruck concentration camp, a notorious women's death camp. The appalling conditions in the camp, including forced labor, rat-infested barracks, malnutrition, and disease, did not deter the sisters' confidence in a God of joy and love. Twice a day Corrie led Bible studies with her Bible that miraculously went unseen by the guards. Betsie had a vision that after the war they would travel all over the world telling people what God had taught them in the camp, "that the light of Jesus is stronger than the deepest darkness." But Betsie didn't live to see her dream; she died in late 1944. Because of a clerical error, Corrie was released on January 1, 1945.

Corrie soon began to carry out Betsie's dream. For 33 years she traveled to 64 countries, "a tramp for the Lord." Speaking to millions of people, she told them that "there is no pit so deep that the love of Jesus Christ is not deeper still." She spoke at Billy Graham crusades and soon became a household word through her appearances and her many books.

Serve Others

Part of lifestyle evangelism is helping others with a servant heart. When you go on a missions trip, teach Vacation Bible School, deliver food to the homebound, teach literacy classes, or serve food at a soup kitchen, you are showing that Christ's call on your life has led you to serve others. You can use these opportunities to witness with both your actions and your words.

WITNESSING LASTS A LIFETIME

Personal witnessing should be a spiritual discipline that we practice every day of our lives for the rest of our lives.

John Harper, a native of Scotland, was a wonderful example of a Christian who witnessed to others until his dying moment. He preached at Chicago's Moody Church in 1911 and was invited back the next year when the church was searching for a new pastor. He sailed on the *Titanic* and was one of the people who went down with the ship. Before his death in the icy waters, he witnessed to a young sailor asking him, "Are you saved?" and quoting Scripture to him. The sailor was rescued and later professed faith in Christ telling everyone, "I am John Harper's last convert."

WITNESSING IS A PROCESS

The Bible teaches that sharing the gospel with others involves a process. For example, 1 Corinthians 3:6 records how Paul planted the seed and Apollos watered it.

Some people are reluctant to respond to a Christian witness. They feel that they don't need God because they are moral enough already, are not good enough for Him to accept them, or don't believe in the existence of a God. When this happens, continue nurturing your friendship with that person and call on God in prayer about the situation.

When Lettie Kirkpatrick first met Wendy, she assumed Wendy was a Christian; after all, they were both attending a writers conference for Christians. She soon learned, through the course of driving together to the conference, that Wendy was not a believer.

"On the ride home, Wendy commented that the conference was great, but she'd never been around so many 'church people.' I had my opening!" says Lettie. "I said, 'Wendy, are you a believer? Have you ever asked Christ to come into your life?' She quickly responded, 'No, I've got too many questions about this church stuff.' Enthusiastically I blurted, 'Wendy, do you realize how much God loves you to draw you to a place like this and then to plant you in our car for the ride? And it's not about church, it's about a relationship with Jesus."

Wendy said she was unable to make a decision at that moment, and so began a witnessing relationship between the two women. Lettie has shared books and tapes with Wendy; she's invited her to Christian events; and they've attended the writers conference together for 4 years now. Still, Wendy has not accepted Christ.

Lettie says the experience has taught her to wait upon the Lord while she's waiting on Wendy to make a decision. "God has taught me about His heart for Wendy and His power to plant people, circumstances, and truth in the lives of our loved ones," she says. "I am clearly reminded that I am not the only one waiting on Wendy."

THE ULTIMATE REWARD OF PERSONAL WITNESSING

The salvation of just one person is a cause for complete celebration, so rejoice! "'There is rejoicing in the presence of the angels of God over one sinner who repents,'" Luke 15:10 records Jesus as saying.

"There is no joy more exquisite than the joy of leading a person to Christ. . . . It is the joy of angels, setting all the harps of heaven to ringing," said A. B. Simpson (1844–1919), founder of the Christian and Missionary Alliance. "Let the cords of love be lengthened and used to draw men and women to Christ. Let our efforts for His kingdom reach a wider circle. Let us make the world our parish. . . . Let us never rest until it is fully known in every corner of the world." Simpson did his part to spread the gospel; by 1897 his missionary organization had sent out 350 missionaries.

May we follow in Simpson's footsteps and continue his legacy. . . . May we yearn to share our faith and joy with others. . . . May we become devoted and disciplined today as a true witness of Christ.

PERSONAL QUESTIONS ABOUT PERSONAL WITNESSING

- Have I thanked God recently for my salvation?
- Do I have a fear of witnessing? Have I tried to conquer that fear?
- Do I pray regularly for those who are not believers?
- Am I aware of or have I participated in witness training sessions?
- Is my lifestyle a witness?
- Did someone see Jesus in me today?

MAKING PERSONAL WITNESSING A PART OF YOUR LIFE

- Thank God right now for your salvation through Christ.
- Ask God for opportunities to witness daily.
- Write down the names of five people whom you know are not Christians. Pray diligently for them.
- Go somewhere today that you usually don't go, such as a self-service

laundry or a park. Be attentive to the needs of people you meet and be open to witnessing opportunities.

- Attend a witnessing seminar at your church
- Read biographies of people whose lives have been transformed through the love of Christ (John Wesley, Dwight Moody, Corrie ten Boom, Billy Graham, and others).
- Sing or meditate upon well-known evangelistic hymns such as "We've a Story to Tell" and "Share His Love." They inspire us to share salvation with others.
- Share books that witness of God's transforming power.
- Watch the *Jesus* film with an unbeliever.
- Write letters or emails that will encourage an unbeliever.
- Reach out to someone you know who needs to trust God by being his or her friend, being a good listener, inviting him or her to your house, etc.
- Pray daily for those who are not Christians.
- Pray daily for missionaries.
- Record your testimony in writing.
- If you don't feel an urgency to share your faith, talk to God about it. Pray that He will give you a desire and ability to share in your own special way.

LIFE APPLICATION VERSE

"'You will receive power when the Holy Spirit comes on you; and you will be my witnesses in Jerusalem, and in all Judea and Samaria, and to the ends of the earth'" (Acts 1:8).

PRAYER

Thank You, God, that You have provided for our salvation through Christ. Thank You for the privilege that I have to witness. I pray for all who do not know You as Savior. Empower me to be an articulate, joyful witness for You in everything I say and do. Amen.

5
SOLITUDE

"Solitude is essential if your roots are to grow deep."—Anne Ortlund, author of *Disciplines of the Heart*

"Find rest, O my soul, in God alone; my hope comes from him. He alone is my rock and my salvation; he is my fortress, I will not be shaken" (Psalm 62:5–6).

Christian comedian Chonda Pierce is often surrounded by people. She has performed before thousands on the Women of Faith tour, at Billy Graham evangelistic crusades and the Grand Ole Opry, and on her own stand-up tours. She revels in the laughs and ovations of packed churches and auditoriums.

Chonda says, though, that it's moments of solitude that help keep her anchored. "A cool morning, a cup of coffee with French vanilla cream, a good John Ortberg book, and my Bible at the kitchen table. Now, that's heavenly!" she says. "I also love the garden in my backyard when the weeds haven't hidden the bench beside the bird bath."

Solitude, she says, helps keep the rest of her life in perspective. Her silent time alone with God gives her strength and the proper attitude to perform the various jobs in her life.

"Every time I step out on a platform and face a sea of faces, I am reminded that my time alone with God is imperative. Every time my kids ask me a question about something weighing on their minds, I am reminded that time alone with God was imperative," Chonda reflects. "It's all about preparation. Time alone with God is preparation for the days to come. Time alone with God is also the building of my relationship with Him."

Like many busy Christian women today, Chonda is often challenged to cultivate more moments of solitude with God. When she's on tour, she finds plenty of time to be alone with God: when her crew is setting up the stage, when she's riding down some anonymous road in her tour bus, or when she's sitting in a quiet hotel room. She is often challenged, though, to make that time quality time.

"It's easy for an undisciplined person like me to flip the channels on the TV, play cards on the computer. I have found if I don't spend some silent time with God, I will NOT survive the isolation of the road," she explains. "It is absolutely a matter of survival. The great thing is, while I'm trying to 'survive,' God is growing me up. Our relationship moves to a more intimate level because of our time together."

The spiritual discipline of solitude (the act of withdrawing to be alone in order to follow spiritual pursuits such as prayer, listening to God, reading, writing, and fasting) is absolutely essential. In a world filled with noise and busyness, Christians must make it a priority to connect with God in a silent, contemplative way. Only in spending time with God in solitude can we hear His voice; and only then can we go back into the world with the proper perspective and preparedness.

In her book *The Velveteen Woman*, Brenda Waggoner calls this time of solitude with God couch time.

"If we want a quality relationship with God, we [need to] spend some 'couch time' each day cultivating it," she says. "We need to set aside quality time to commune with God regularly. Time to ask God to search our hearts, to see His smile, feel His comfort, and know His approval. . . . If we are to be transformed . . . , we'll have to pull up a chair and visit, linger a while, and get to know Him personally, not just learn *about* Him."

WHY DO WE NEED SOLITUDE?

"My soul finds rest in God alone," wrote the psalmist (Psalm 62:1). In spending time in solitude and silence with God, our souls find the only true rest they can obtain. Solitude truly does wonders for our relationship with our Savior.

Thomas à Kempis (1379?–1471), in his classic *The Imitation of Christ,* wrote, "Shut thy door upon thee, and call unto thyself Jesus thy beloved. Remain with Him in thy chamber, for thou shalt not elsewhere find so great peace."

We must make it a priority to replenish ourselves spiritually by withdrawing from the busyness of life. We often neglect this need for solitude simply because our lives make it nearly impossible. They are too filled with activities, noises, stresses, and to-do lists.

By choosing solitude (instead of the never-ending rush from place to place), we have time to listen to God, commune with Him, develop a deeper relationship with Him, adore Him, contemplate Him, thank Him, and enjoy Him.

Solitude also allows us time to study the Bible and pray, to meditate, to become recharged and energized, to worship privately, to deal with the stresses of everyday life and the difficulties during bleak times, and to seek guidance and direction.

Mary An Wilson, a minister of worship and spiritual formation who attends silent retreats and practices solitude daily, says the discipline has truly changed her life.

"In silence and solitude, we hear more and more of God's voice. We are able to follow more and more of God's leadership in our lives. We know more and more of the peace and joy of God," she says. "I am aware of being connected to the Spirit of God in others. I am aware of being in God's Spirit even in the grandest chaos—of which there is plenty in my life."

Wife, mother, and writer Susan Titus Osborn remembers the moment when she realized she needed to spend more time in silence and solitude. She sat in a chair on the beach near her home, wondering why her life felt so unfulfilling. "I rushed from one activity to another, never feeling a sense of accomplishment. Was I always too busy *doing* to take time to enjoy God's gifts to me?" she remembers asking. "I bowed my head and said a silent prayer, asking God to slow me down."

At that moment, she says, "A sense of God's peace" rolled in with the waves. She realized that "God's voice is often a whisper. We must slow down and be silent to hear Him speak to us. Only then can He show us His will for each moment of our lives."

Perhaps Lettie B. Cowman put it best in her classic book *Streams in the Desert*: "To be left alone with Him is a foretaste of heaven."

MODELS OF SOLITUDE

The Bible provides us with many models of solitude. The first couple walked and talked with God alone in the garden. Great men and women of the Bible sought time alone. Moses was alone when he met God in the burning bush. Jacob, Elijah, and Elisha spent time alone with God. Cornelius was alone when the angel came to him (Acts 10:2). Peter was alone on the housetop when God told him to go to the Gentiles (Acts 10:9). John the Baptist was alone in the wilderness, Paul was alone on the Damascus Road, and John was alone on the Isle of Patmos.

Jesus is our best model for solitude. Jesus was drawn to solitude. The Gospels often record Him withdrawing from the crowds.

Why did Jesus need to be alone? Why did He have to get away sometimes from His disciples? What did He do alone that He couldn't do with people? He prayed. He listened to the Father. He sought direction and guidance. He refreshed Himself. He received strength and wisdom.

The Gospels give us these indications of the importance of solitude in the life of Jesus:

"After He [Jesus] had dismissed them, He went up into the hills by Himself to pray. When evening came, He was there alone" (Matt. 14:23).

"Very early in the morning, while it was still dark, Jesus got up, left the house and went off to a solitary place, where He prayed" (Mark 1:35).

"But Jesus often withdrew to lonely places and prayed" (Luke 5:16).

A TIME AND PLACE FOR SOLITUDE

We can see that solitude is important, but how can we practice it in a practical way in our lives today? One of the most important ways to make it a priority is to find a special time and place for moments of solitude.

We must find a method to quiet our soul, just as the psalmist advises us: "But I have calmed and quieted my soul, like a child quieted at its mother's breast; like a child that is quieted is my soul" (Psalm 131:2).

Anselm (1033–1109), the archbishop of Canterbury, extolled the importance of time and place. "Flee for a while from your tasks, hide yourself for a little space from the turmoil of your thoughts," he said. "For a little while give your time to God, and rest in him for a little while."

Susanna Wesley (1669–1742) took Anselm's advice. The mother of 19 children, she set aside time from her many household tasks to be alone with God. The mother of John, the founder of Methodism, and Charles, the great hymnwriter, she designated two hours daily for private devotion. This time alone with God strengthened her as she faced adversities including the deaths of 10 of her children, family debts, the burning of her home, and the death of her husband.

Thomas Kinkade, a popular Christian watercolor artist, believes it's important to find a special place for retreat and refuge. "Your corner of peace may be as simple as a comfortable chair with an old-fashioned lamp beside it. You turn on the lamp and sink into the chair in the circle of warm light," he says.

Kinkade says that the specifics of the place aren't really important. "Your place of retreat, your little corner of peace, may be very different from mine. The specifics don't really matter," he says. "The point is you find a place that gives your senses a chance to unwind and lets you catch a fresh vision of peacetime possibilities."

WHAT TAKES PLACE DURING TIMES OF SOLITUDE?

Perhaps you're wondering what a time of solitude and silence *looks* like. What do you during this time? Many possibilities exist.

Pray and listen to God. When we practice solitude, we are more attuned to God's voice in prayer.

Author Brenda Waggoner says that prayer "becomes a space of uncluttered rest" when done in silence. It becomes a "two-way conversation" and a "time to listen carefully," she says.

The renowned African American missionary evangelist Amanda Smith (1837–1915) was a great woman of prayer. Often alone, she prayed everywhere. Whether it was beside an old trunk, under an apple tree, or beside a log, she prayed thanking God for the simplest blessings and asking Him for direction. Once she even prayed when she found herself swept into a ditch by a cold wind. Asking God to still the wind, it stopped. She evangelized in England, India, and Africa. All the finances for her trips were the results of answered prayers.

Read the Bible. Can you truly pay attention to what God is telling you through His Word if you're reading it with noise and distractions around you? You can best hear God's voice through His Word when you read it in solitude.

Meditate. Rather just than reading the Bible, meditate on it. Meditation cannot really happen apart from solitude and silence. Take time to meditate on one word (*Jesus, Redeemer, grace*), a verse ("In the beginning was the Word, and the Word was with God, and the Word was God" [John 1:1]), or a chapter (Psalm 23). What does it mean to you? How is God speaking to you through it?

Henri J. M. Nouwen, the author of *Out of Solitude: Three Meditations on the Christian Life*, said, "In solitude we can listen to the voice of him who spoke to us before we could speak a word, who healed us before we could make any gesture to help, who set us free long before we could free others, and who loved us long before we could give love to anyone."

Journal. Spend time in solitude as an opportunity to write your thoughts, reflections, prayers, and meditations. This unencumbered, undistracted time is the perfect opportunity to do so.

Fast. Christians throughout the centuries have sought solitude to fast and concentrate on spiritual matters. Jesus was alone when led "by the Spirit into the wilderness to be tempted by the devil. He fasted forty days and forty nights" (Matt. 4:1–2).

The great Italian mystic Catherine of Genoa (1447–1510) practiced fasting for almost 23 years. Prayer and fasting only seemed to strengthen her as she became active in humanitarian activities. Director of the St. Lazarus hospital in Genoa from 1490 to 1496, she nursed many when the plague broke out in 1493.

Seek guidance. In solitude, we can hear God's voice as He guides us in the direction we should go. While a young man, the great prophet

Samuel was alone when God spoke to him calling, "Samuel! Samuel!" In obedience, Samuel proclaimed: "Speak, for your servant is listening" (1 Sam. 3:10).

Enjoy God's creation. The English poet Elizabeth Barrett Browning (1806–1861) said it well: "Earth's crammed with heaven. And every common bush afire with God." Often when we are outdoors, at the beach, in the mountains, or in our backyard, we find strength in solitude.

For author (and wife of famed navigator Charles Lindbergh) Anne Morrow Lindbergh (1907–2001), it was the seashore. She wrote her classic book *Gifts from the Sea* while alone there. "I find there is a quality to being alone that is incredibly precious," she wrote. "Life rushes back into the void, richer, more vivid, fuller than before."

Worship. Use moments of solitude and silence to worship God with praise, love, and adoration. Author Anita Corrine Donihue says, "In silence, I give You praise and wait so You can minister to me."

While vacationing in China, Rosiland Rinker, author of such books as *Prayer: Conversing with God,* saw Chinese women worship meaningless idols and came away from the experience with a new appreciation for true worship. She rushed out of the temple, compelled to worship God right then and there. "I wanted to go into my own room and close the door. . . . I wanted to be quiet and let all the love and adoration and worship of my heart go out to Him in a way that I had never done before," she remembers. "I have learned that it is in holy silence, that my heart pours out its best love and worship to God."

Sing hymns or praise choruses. Use your time of solitude to sing your love and praises to God (even if you can only make a "joyful noise"!).

Read Christian literature. Not only can you spend your times of solitude in reading the Bible; you can also read Christian classics, devotional books, or Christian novels. In silence you will better appreciate the words you are reading.

Be silent. Sometimes we need to not be only alone but be silent to listen to God. Mother Teresa said, "The religious need silence to hear God speak to them." She believed there could be no life of prayer without silence.

Author and speaker Shelia Walsh says, "When I'm quiet, life falls into perspective for me. I have a very active mind and I'm a worrier, but in those moments when I choose to put that away, I rest beside the Shepherd in still places."

Mary An Wilson says that silence is the integral part of her moments with God. "Silence is all about listening to God. I learned in teaching young children that if they are talking all the time, they can never hear what I have to say. Is it not the same with God? If I go to God with my praises and my requests and my confessions (all of which are essential ingredients) and then I say "Amen" and go on with my busy day, do I not leave God saying, 'But wait, child, I have some things to say to you as well'?" she says. "If I have 20 minutes, I am going to dispense altogether with MY talking and simply sit in silence—setting aside all the sounds and ideas that invade my silence as best I can."

Mary An takes these daily "retreats" into silence at her home each day. "I go into silence seeking God's voice and to see more clearly where God is moving in my life, to discern where God wants me to be at that moment in time. I have never been disappointed!" she says.

Ecclesiastes 3:7 reminds us that there is "a time to be silent." We need to seek that time often.

RESULTS OF SOLITUDE

When Philip Yancey, author of such popular Christian books as *What's So Amazing About Grace?* and *The Bible Jesus Read*, turned 50 he underwent a complete physical checkup. He decided to also undergo a spiritual checkup, enrolling in a silent retreat; the result, he says, was a renewed desire to grow spiritually.

"In those days of silence and solitude, I paid attention to what I might need to change in order to keep my soul in shape. The more I listened, the longer grew the list," he recalls. "From my doctor, I learned that no matter what I do my body will continue to deteriorate. At best, a good diet and exercise routine will slow that deterioration. Spiritually, however, I can look forward to growth, renewed vigor, and improved health—as long as I continue to listen, and then act on what I hear God saying."

Your times of solitude and silence, whether they come in a daily form or in a planned retreat like Yancey's, offer you many opportunities to grow as a Christian. The results can be varied, but will all be life-changing.

A deeper spiritual life. Imagine if all Christians followed the admonition of the psalmist: "Be still, and know that I am God" (Psalm 46:10). Can you now picture the depth of spirituality we would see in the lives of Christians everywhere? Can you imagine how much closer to God we would all be?

"If His followers spent more time alone with Him, we would have spiritual giants again," said Lettie B. Cowman.

Madame Guyon (1648–1717) was one of those spiritual giants. A Catholic, she influenced many Protestants and continues to do so. Methodist John Wesley (1703–1791) said of her, "We may search many centuries before we find another woman who was such a pattern of true holiness." American Baptist missionary Adoniram Judson (1788–1850), while serving 21 months in a vermin-infested prison in Burma, tried to imitate Madame Guyon's meek acquiescence by repeating her verses: "No bliss I seek, but to fulfill / In life, in death, thy lovely will."

The writer of 40 books and a 20-volume commentary on the Bible, Madame Guyon spent 7 years in and out of prison, the last 4 years in solitary confinement in the infamous Bastille in Paris. Sentenced by Louis XIV for her religious beliefs, she displayed a triumphant inner spirit writing: "My prison walls can not control / The flight, the freedom of my soul."

Ability to concentrate, imagine, and create. Many creative works have been borne from solitude.

English author John Bunyan (1628–1688) wrote his famous *Pilgrim's Progress* in prison with only his Bible and *Foxe's Book of Martyrs.* The classic has sold millions and has been translated into hundreds of languages.

Fanny Crosby composed many of her hymns after midnight when she was alone with her thoughts. She wrote 8,000 hymns.

Simpler lives. Nurse and author Jane E. Maxwell discovered that periods of solitude could "simplify my life as they simplified my harried mind and calmed my anxious spirit." She goes on to say in *God's Abundance* that "periods of solitude stretch my time. . . . I can clear my mind, focus on the important things, and see God's pattern . . . by simplifying, I am actually more effective."

Preparation for service. After Jesus began His day in solitude, He went out to serve. Countless Christians since Him have practiced the same method: spend time in solitude and silence with God, then go out into the world to serve Him.

English Baptist minister Charles Spurgeon said, "We should be better Christians if we were more alone, waiting upon God, and gathering through meditation on His Word spiritual strength for labor in His service."

Antony of Egypt (251–356), the founder of Christian monasticism, withdrew at the age of 35 into absolute solitude. On a mountain near the Nile River, he lived in an old fort for 20 years before some of his disciples convinced him to break his solitude and give them spiritual leadership. When he joined them, they were surprised to find his mind and body in vigorous condition. He spent the rest of his life with his group of monks in the desert. He sporadically left to help the needy, encourage Christians in prison, and preach. He lived to be 105.

From the ages of 14 to 17, Catherine of Siena (1347–1380) spent 3 years in solitary communion with God. This preparation of fasting and praying readied her for a life of service. She ministered to the sick and dying during the Black Death that swept Europe in 1374. She lost ten family members.

Working for the reformation of the Catholic Church, she prayed as many as six hours each day for the restoration for the church from its corruption to its original purity. She wrote almost 400 letters addressed to kings, popes, and church leaders. She was influential in returning the papacy from France to Rome. Her exemplary life led a biographer to say, "No Christian woman has surpassed Catherine of Siena in sacrifice and devotion."

MAKING IT A PRIORITY

Andrew Murray (1828–1917), missionary leader/devotional writer, challenges us in his classic book *Abide in Christ*: "May each one of us learn every day to say, 'Truly my soul is silent unto God.'"

Andrew Murray was right. His words still apply today. Solitude is a neglected discipline. It is not natural to us; we, instead, tend to think in terms of how much we can get done in a day, how many activities we can complete, how many places we can go. Solitude and silence, though, are extremely important if we want to grow closer to God and grow more Christlike in our daily walk.

Mary An Wilson says that we must make spending time with God and listening to Him the utmost priorities in our lives. "How can we be in the center of God's will if we 'don't have time' to LISTEN," she says. "We are busy DOING what we perceive to be God's will. But God calls us to simply BE first of all. Then we will know what to DO."

PERSONAL QUESTIONS ABOUT SOLITUDE

- Am I practicing solitude daily?
- Do I feel a need to be alone?
- Is my day so filled with schedules and to-do lists that I do not take the time to be alone with God?
- If I am not spending time alone, what keeps me from practicing solitude?
- Is the fear of being alone keeping me from thinking and meditating on God?
- Am I too involved in activities that I fear being alone?
- Do I have a special place and time that I can be alone?

MAKING SOLITUDE A PART OF YOUR LIFE

- Find a favorite place where you can be alone without any interruptions. It may be in a comfortable chair or under your favorite tree.
- Carve out a specific time that you will use for solitude and silence.
- Use your time alone to meditate, pray, sing praise songs, and write in your spiritual journal.

• Use your time alone to recharge and get ready for the day or tasks ahead of you.
• Think of taking solitary moments as vacations—take 15-minute or even 30-minute "vacations" during the day.
• Try to arrange solitary moments (snippets of solitude) of peace and quiet during the day. Go for a walk, turn off the TV, unplug the computer.
• If you have children at home, find a way to make time for solitude.
• Consider going to a monastery or spiritual retreat for a time of intense spiritual solitude. (Several monasteries are open to laypeople and have reasonable rates.)
• For a week, meditate on Psalm 46:10.
• Spend a half day alone with God several times a year. Pray for guidance; ask God to help you set your goals for the upcoming months; pray for others.
• Consider fasting a few times a year.
• Be still and in silence listen to God for 15 minutes a day.
• Engage yourself in a "spiritual checkup." After spending this time in solitude, ask yourself: What spiritual lessons have I learned? How can I grow closer to Christ?

LIFE APPLICATION VERSE

"Be still, and know that I am God" (Psalm 46:10).

PRAYER

Forgive us, O God, for not spending more time in silence with You. Too often we seek to crowd both You and the world out of our lives with noise. Have mercy on us for neglecting what peace there is in quietude. Rescue us from the escapism of noise. Teach us to pursue peace and solitude that we may be more present to You, finding great delight and consolation in Your holy presence. Let us turn to You in stillness, that filled with quiet renewal we may face the world anew. In Jesus' name we pray. Amen.

6

JOURNALING

"Journaling makes me feel like a spider who is constantly pulling out its thread and creating a beautiful web picture."—Luci Shaw, author and leader of journaling workshops

"Let this be written for a future generation, that a people not yet created may praise the Lord" (Psalm 102:18).

Because he feared the rising power of Christianity, the Roman emperor Septimius Severus issued an edict prohibiting Christians from teaching or making converts. Vibia Perpetua (181?–203) was condemned a short time after her baptism. She was thrown into prison; and when allowed to keep her infant son, wrote, "Immediately I gained strength and being relieved from my anxiety about the child, my prison suddenly became to me a palace, so that I preferred to be there rather than anywhere else." When questioned about whether she was a Christian, she said, "I am. I cannot forsake my faith for freedom." She was thrown into an area with wild beasts and then beheaded. An early Christian martyr, she recorded her experiences up until the day of her death.

If Vibia had not written about (journaled) her experiences, we would not know about her willingness to sacrifice her life for her faith.

Sixteen centuries later Ann Judson (1789–1826), the first woman missionary to the Far East, informed and inspired a generation of Americans about overseas missions. Through her letters and journals, she wrote gripping accounts of the problems of Burmese women and appealed for women's work there: "Let us make a united effort . . . to instruct to enlighten and save females in the Eastern world."

The leading female missionary author of the early nineteenth century also revealed in her journal her close walk with God. Ann wrote soon before marrying Adoniram and sailing for Burma, "When I am called to face danger, to pass through scenes of terror and distress, He can inspire me with fortitude, and enable me to trust in Him." These words proved prophetic, for Ann suffered greatly in her 14 years of service. She lost a child and constantly battled diseases. When Adoniram was arrested and imprisoned for 21 months in a vermin-infested prison, she moved nearby regularly ministering to him and nursing him through fevers. Her health deteriorated, and she died shortly afterward.

Like Vibia and Ann, Christians throughout history have recorded their innermost thoughts. Some of the most famous people of all time have kept journals: nurse Florence Nightingale; scientist Blaise Pascal; Puritan clergyman Cotton Mather; missionaries Mother Teresa, Jim Elliot, Amy Carmichael, David Brainerd, David Livingstone, Mary Slessor, and Henry Martyn; Quaker founder George Fox; colonial minister Jonathan Edwards; evangelist George Whitefield; Methodist founder John Wesley; minister Charles Spurgeon; abolitionists John Woolman and Sojourner Truth; revivalist Charles Finney; author Leo Tolstoy; orphanage founder George Mueller; Salvation Army founder William Booth. The list could go on and on.

Many Christians today continue the tradition of journal writing. They use journals in a myriad of ways: to record their activities and thoughts, to keep track of their prayers, to enjoy a time of solitude and silence. And, in doing so, they often find opportunities to draw closer to God.

WHAT IS JOURNALING?

Journaling (the practice of writing down your thoughts, meditations, praises, and prayers) can be a powerful spiritual discipline. Writing can be God-inspired as it was for Jeremiah when the Lord told him to "take a scroll and write on it all the words I have spoken to you" (Jer. 36:1–2).

The word *journal* originally came from the Latin word, *diurnalis*, meaning daily. The Middle English word *journal* referred to a daily service book containing the religious services to be said at different times during the day.

WHY JOURNAL?

Christians have journaled throughout the ages and continue to do so today for many reasons.

A simple pleasure. Journaling is one of those simple pleasures of life. With a journal, one has a best friend, a confidant. In a solitary and soul-searching way, journaling helps us turn inward and experience inner growth, self-discovery, and self-reflection. We make a daily discovery of where we are in our spiritual journey.

Valuable solitary time. Journaling provides valuable solitary time in our lives when we are able to meditate and have special encounters with God.

Lynn D. Morrissey, a CLASS (Christian Leadership and Speaking Services) speaker who leads seminars on prayer journaling, says that journaling provides a way for us to spend solitary, unhurried moments with God. "You spend more time in the Father's presence," she says. "Journaling is a great vehicle to enjoying intimacy with God."

An analytical look at our lives. "The desire to record and reflect upon one's life seems to be an almost instinctual human need," says author Morton T. Kelsey in *Adventure Inward: Christian Growth Through Personal Journal Writing.*

Even Job, one of the great men of the Old Testament, wished that his words would last: "Oh, that my words were recorded, that they were written on a scroll, that they were inscribed with an iron tool on lead, or engraved in rock forever! I know that my Redeemer lives, and that in the end He will stand upon the earth" (Job 19:23–25).

Abolitionist John Woolman (1720–1772) used his journal as a tool to look analytically and introspectively at his life. His *Journal* has been called "a classic in American literature and a devotional manual of enduring power." Beginning his journal, he wrote, "I have often felt a motion of love to leave some hints in writing of my experience of the goodness of God, and now, in the thirty-sixth year of my age, I begin this work." Woolman would maintain the journal throughout his life.

Luci Shaw, a writer-in-residence at Regent University in Vancouver, Canada, and popular speaker on journaling, says that she first journaled after her husband was diagnosed with lung cancer. The illness forced her to look analytically at her life. "The emotional and physical upheaval, and the existential questions his illness caused in me, suggested that this was a time of enormous transition in our lives," she remembers. "I was asking huge questions, praying with great intensity, and absorbing lessons in faith so fast that I knew the whole experience would be lost in a blur of memory if I didn't begin to record it on a daily basis."

A record of our spiritual life. Journals are an excellent way to record our spiritual life for ourselves, our children, or for later generations of Christians. Edna Ellison, a former magazine editor and grandmother, journals because it's a way of transmitting her legacy of faith. "A journal is a treasured history where you can pass along your legacy, as God's people have done for centuries."

Many famous Christians in our history have recorded their spiritual journeys. The great colonial minister Jonathan Edwards penned: "On January 12, 1723, I made a solemn dedication of myself to God, and wrote it down; giving up myself, and all that I had to God."

Edwards later would publish the journal of David Brainerd (1718–1747), missionary to the Native American Indians, who lived only 29 years, but through his diary influenced countless others. His life inspired missionaries such as English Baptist William Carey; Methodist Thomas Coke, Bible translator to China Robert Morrison, Anglican Henry Martyn, English Samuel Marsden, American Samuel Mills, and Scottish Thomas Chalmers. *The Life and Diary of David Brainerd* is still published today.

Methodist founder John Wesley wrote in his journal about his conversion at a meeting in London's Aldersgate Street: "I felt my heart strangely warmed. I felt I did trust in Christ, Christ alone for salvation."

Jim Elliot (1927–1956), missionary to the Auca Indians, began his journal while at Wheaton College. The record of his spiritual growth contained many memorable quotes that still influence people today:

"He is no fool who gives what he cannot keep to gain what he cannot lose."

"Live to the hilt every situation you believe to be the will of God."

"Consume my life, my God, for it is Thine. I seek not a long life, but a full one, like you, Lord Jesus."

After the Aucas killed Elliot and four of his fellow missionaries in 1956, his journal was published. It influenced many to become missionaries, and countless other readers drew inspiration from a life that was totally given over to God.

Reminder of how far we have come. Keeping a journal can be a reminder of where God has led you in the past. By writing and then remembering such things as an answered prayer, kind words and deeds done for you, a special hymn or Bible verse, a special time when God led you in the right direction, we also can see where God led us out of despair and into hope.

Lori Dickerson, a pediatric nurse and mother, kept a journal during a time in her life when she battled clinical depression. Today she can look back at her journal entries and see how far she has come. "Most of the time it is very difficult to detect the small steps of progress made; but if those steps are recorded, one can look back over them and see how the small steps have become large strides," she says.

Creative outlet. Journal writing can also help us tap into our creative side by putting prayers into writing, creating spiritual poetry, or collecting our thoughts in other creative ways.

Luci Shaw says that journal writing has always been a form of creative expression for her. "My journal is my 'collection jar' for ideas, images, snatches of conversation, content for essays, sermon notes, connections that I see between seen and unseen worlds—all of it is in there. My poems nearly all begin on my journal pages," she explains.

The creative process often uncovers hidden thoughts and concerns. "Once pen touches paper, the ideas start to flow and I begin to write things I never knew I knew," she says.

Self-expression, easing stress, and bringing healing. Lynn Morrissey says she began prayer journaling during a crisis situation, quite by accident. "I was experiencing difficulty with a co-worker who was bent on getting me fired. Out of sheer frustration and fear, every day I'd leave the airport where I worked and go to a restaurant for lunch, taking my journal with me," she remembers. "On its blank notebook pages I began writing out all my frustrations. Before I knew it, the most curious thing happened. I began crying out to God by writing things like 'Dear God, help me in this situation,' and 'Dear God, what should I do?' I became so excited about the process of written prayer that I would set my alarm every morning for 4:30 A.M. and go onto my front porch to write my love letters to God. Although the woman didn't leave our office for over a year, it no longer mattered to me. Because I was meeting with God daily in my journal, I was now experiencing peace in this situation."

Lori Dickerson says she can now read back over her journal entries and see how they helped her in her battle with depression. "The poems and meditations I wrote during this time reflect the depth of emotion I was feeling while in the midst of the despair. I don't think I could have written with that kind of clarity after having come through the trials," she says. "Recording them gave me a chance to return to those healing thoughts whenever encountering those difficult times again."

BENEFITS OF JOURNALING

Lynn Morrissey puts in perspective the benefits of journaling for Christians. She says, "For many Christians such as I once was, they are prayerless and powerless because they have tremendous difficulty praying aloud or silently. They often do not know what to say or how to say it. They often lose focus, and their prayers trail off into oblivion. The simple process of writing allows them to concentrate perhaps for the first time. It miraculously frees them to express themselves. For reasons that I do not quite understand, the writing process encourages cathartic release of emotions. Quite often people who cannot express themselves orally find that when they write, a floodgate of emotions is released and they are finally free to converse with God."

Luci Shaw knows that journaling was God's way of helping her make it through her husband's cancer diagnosis and later death. She specifically remembers the morning she woke up from a dream several months after Harold's death; she raced to her journal.

"As I wrote it, its significance became apparent. In the dream, Harold was meeting me at the airport after I'd been away. We walked out to the parking lot, and he handed me the car keys, saying 'Drive.' This gave me the permission I needed to begin to make decisions and choices about my life, the kind of decisions he had made, or we had made together, before his death. It was a tremendous relief and challenge," she says. "If I hadn't written it down, I doubt if I would have known the dream's significance."

TYPES OF JOURNALING

There are many methods of journaling Christians can pursue. As Luci Shaw points out, "There are almost as many ways of keeping journals as there are journal keepers. Each individual must find her individual style and method that works for her."

Diary Journaling. This type of journal records the daily happenings in an individual's life. The journaler takes the time every day to keep track of the moments, both big and small, that are meaningful to her.

Luci Shaw says this is her most important method of journaling. "I keep a chronological journal of everything significant in my life whether it be spiritual, emotional, artistic, humorous (it helps me to remember good jokes), informational, or simply event-oriented," she says. "I date my entries and note the page numbers for future reference, since rereading old journals has proved as helpful and important in assessing my life and growth as the writing of the present journal."

Kindergarten teacher and mother Gina Jackson keeps what she calls a calendar journal, noting important events and milestones on a daily basis. "I write down important things about the kids, whether it's their getting their tonsils out or having a first sleepover; and family things such as money matters, job-related activities, and health matters. I keep the calendars and refer back to them," she says. "I have even written about weather items such as when flowers bloom or when the drought season starts or when the cool weather starts and the crickets come in."

Prayer Journaling. "Prayer journaling," says Lynn Morrissey, "is writing word-for-word exactly what I would say to God verbally or silently. I call it writing love letters to God, as this allows me the freedom to express anything on my heart to the Lover of my soul. When I write a letter to the Lord, I write simply and unpretentiously anything that is on my heart, realizing that nothing is too insignificant or burdensome to share with Jesus. I used to have difficulty praying because I was trying to emulate pastors whose prayers were very eloquent and flowery. Writing in my own words about real-life situations freed me to express what was on my heart."

Author Kathy Collard Miller also journals her prayers. "My prayertime is so essential and precious to me," she says. "I journal just about all my prayers, and it really helps me to concentrate and hear God's voice. Sometimes, I'll even write down what I hear God saying to me. Most of the time it's the most loving things possible; but even when He chastises me, His voice is gentle and encouraging."

Prayer Request Journal. Another journal method is to record prayer requests and the subsequent answers to those prayers. This helps the journaler keep track of the concerns in his or her life and in the lives of others, and it makes the Christian's prayer life more efficient and effective.

Gina Jackson began keeping track of her prayer requests and answers in 1994. "I keep my prayer list, and make it specific, and then I write down the answers to the prayers. That is really the exciting part," she explains. "Sometimes, the answer comes so quickly, and sometimes it takes years; and sometimes you don't even know it has been answered until you realize the answer is so totally different than what you thought was best."

She can look back now at a prayer request she first wrote down in 1994 concerning the salvation of a friend from work. "I would witness to her and we would talk about it; I wrote her down as a prayer request for years," she says. "And now she has come to the Lord!"

Bible Study Journal. You may choose to keep a Bible study journal, where you record Bible verses and then summarize the meaning of the passages. You can also write out your reflections of what God is teaching you through the passages. For example, Galatians 5:22 ("The fruit of the Spirit is love, joy, peace, patience, kindness, goodness, faithfulness, gentleness, and self-control") is a verse that is full of meaning and application to our lives.

Gratitude Journal. The psalmist says, "I will give thanks to the Lord with my whole heart; I will tell of all your wonderful deeds" (Psalm 9:1). We are supposed to be continually thankful for God's blessings.

A wonderful way to keep track of these blessings is to keep a gratitude journal. The great missionary-explorer David Livingstone (1813–1873) kept a journal on his treks through Africa to open up the continent for evangelization and trade. In many of his entries he expressed gratitude to God. On March 19, 1873, a year before his death, he wrote, "Thanks to the Almighty Preserver of men for sparing me thus far on the journey of life."

Lori Dickerson says that her "praise journal helps to keep me focused. If I am faithful in keeping it, I find it difficult to stay down for very long when writing about all the blessings God has given me. This has become a particularly effective tool in dealing with the milder depression or when I am tempted to throw myself a pity party."

An Autobiography of Spiritual Growth. Some of the greatest Christian devotional classics are "journal entries" that men and women have made of their spiritual life.

The Confessions of St. Augustine is one of the world's greatest devotional classics. Augustine poured out his heart to God: "How then do I seek Thee, O Lord? For when I seek Thee, my God, I seek a happy life. I will seek Thee, that my soul may live."

A modern classic of modern religious spirituality is Dag Hammarskjöld's intimate journal *Markings.* The former United Nations secretary general recorded deeply personal reflections and asked that his journal not be published until after his death. His musings are inspirational: "Give me a pure heart—that I my see Thee, / A humble heart—that I may hear Thee, / A heart of love—that I my serve Thee / A heart of faith—that I may abide in Thee."

OTHER SPECIAL JOURNALS

Sunday Morning Journal. Some people keep a journal in which they write sermon notes and impressions of the way the Holy Spirit speaks to them during sermons.

Travel Journals. These journals can record impressions of scenic, historic, or religious travels such as those to the Holy Land. People who go on missions trips often keep journals.

Wanda Fontaine kept a journal when she traveled to Mexico in July 2001 for a week as part of a medical team. "As a RN, I was able to use my nursing skills in a mission setting." She received such a blessing from visiting in four sites running a medical clinic seeing 25–75 patients a day. "Approximately 20 percent of the people at our clinics made decisions for Christ," Wanda said. "All the people were willing to accept a copy of a Bible."

Wanda recorded her experiences about the trip in a special journal; she wrote every evening about the events of the day and how they affected her. "I also kept a separate short prayer journal each morning during my quiet time. I would write down a verse that impressed me from my portion of Scripture each morning. I journalized my specific prayer that I prayed that day. It was awesome each day to see the way God answered prayers," she says. "Journaling definitely enhanced my missions experience."

Holiday Journal. Ella Robinson, an administrative assistant and freelance writer, keeps a Christmas journal. "For eight years, I have used Christmas Eve night to reminisce on family and personal events that happened throughout the year," she says. "I have written about gifts my husband and I have given to each other. I've written about my aunt dying before Christmas a few years ago. I've written about the goodies I've baked for friends. One year I wrote about an ice storm that came into the state. It's a great way to remember the holidays."

POWER OF JOURNALING

God convicted Lynn Morrissey of the sin of alcoholism through her journaling. She recalls: "I became very depressed, and a physician suggested that I see a psychiatrist, which raised a red flag for me. I ran to God in His Word and in my journal; and in a matter of three days, He showed me that He, alone, would be my Wonderful Counselor. I felt He was showing me, personally, not to see the psychiatrist. I stopped drinking, cold turkey, and during the painful and difficult days which followed, I ran to my Wonderful Counselor (sometimes several times a day) in my journal. I have no doubt that if I had not prayed, I couldn't have stopped drinking. And if I had not journaled, I wouldn't have prayed because that is virtually the only form of prayer in which I engage with any regularity and success. If I hadn't journaled, I would still be drinking today. That was 15 years ago, and I shudder to think of the condition in which I'd be today—if indeed, I were still even living!"

Edna Ellison remembers using her journal to record her thoughts and fears after a terrible car accident left her young adult son in critical condition. "I had lots of time as I sat in the hospital room alone. One way I passed the time was journaling," she says. "I have been through many dark valleys in my lifetime, and recording my prayers still helps me with bittersweet memories of where I've been and how God shines a light at the end of the tunnel."

Journaling serves many purposes. It can be a way to overcome traumatic events and find healing, a way to discover God's guidance in your life, a way to record your spiritual journey for your children and grandchildren, a way to keep track of your prayers and their answers. It's a wonderful tool for becoming a more disciplined Christian.

In whatever way you use your journal, remember this: "My heart overflows with a good theme; I address my verses to the King. My tongue is the pen of a ready writer" (Psalm 45:1 NASB).

PERSONAL QUESTIONS ABOUT JOURNALING

- Do I journal? If I do, am I satisfied with my method of journaling?
- Do I have a regular time for my journaling or do I journal sporadically?

- Have I ever kept a prayer journal? If not, I'll consider doing so.
- Do I keep a gratitude journal? If not, I'll consider doing so.
- If I do journal, what is God teaching me?
- How has God used my journal to guide me through difficult times?

MAKING JOURNALING PART OF YOUR LIFE

- Find a journal that suits your tastes and needs. It may be a spiral-bound notebook, a ring binder with loose-leaf paper, a blank book, or even a computer. Find a pen with which you can freely record your thoughts.
- Determine the best time to write in your journal. It may be only once a day or it may be several times a day. You may find that you can write just three or four times a week.
- Find a place to be still and quiet and listen to God. It may be in your favorite chair or on your garden bench.
- Begin a journal by listing ways that God has worked in your life.
- Read the journals of famous Christians such as David Brainerd and John Wesley.
- If you are reluctant to keep a journal because you don't want anyone to read it, make sure your will states that your journal will be destroyed upon your death. You might also want to keep your journal locked up.
- If you have trouble getting started, begin by setting a 15-minute time limit.
- If you have writer's block, consider some of these suggestions:
    1. Write letters to Jesus pouring out your feelings as well as praise and thanksgiving.
    2. Write about your conversion experience.
    3. Write about the biblical character you would most want to meet in heaven.
    4. Write about how God has blessed you.
    5. Look in a quotation book and find a favorite quotation and expound on it.

LIFE APPLICATION VERSE

"Let this be written for a future generation, that a people not yet created may praise the Lord" (Psalm 102:18).

PRAYER

Dear Lord, be with me as I begin or continue the discipline of writing love letters to You. I want to write of Your works and of Your blessings. I want to write of and remember the ways You have worked repeatedly in my life. I want to praise You with my creativity and with my pen. In Jesus' name. Amen.

7
Personal Study

"Reading Christians are growing Christians. When Christians cease to read, they cease to grow."—John Wesley, Methodist founder

"An intelligent mind acquires knowledge, and the ear of the wise seeks knowledge" (Prov. 18:15 RSV).

At a time in my life when I had a lot of questions about my faith and about direction in my life, I read *The Hobbit* by J. R. R. Tolkien," says David Copeland, professor of journalism at Elon College in North Carolina. "I learned much from Bilbo who didn't want to go on his journeys to search for the ring. First, I realized, like Bilbo, that we are called to go on journeys to do things that we don't necessarily want to do. Sometimes there are tasks that we are called to do, but we don't understand the calling. Bilbo fought the calling like we do. Sometimes we have to do those things even though we don't understand why." Like Bilbo, David didn't understand a calling to be more involved in his local church and with the young people in his church.

The second lesson David learned from *The Hobbit* was that "God gives us talents, but unless they are channeled into God's work, they don't become spiritual gifts. In *The Hobbit* Bilbo doesn't comprehend that what he is doing is for the greater good, but he does it anyway. What I understand is that we can't know God's plan; but if we hear His calling and follow it, in the end what we have done is of value. It becomes a gift for God. It is always uplifting for us to see the great by-products of our journeys. Bilbo finally saw that he was part of something bigger than himself, and that is what we all need to realize.

"Third, through Tolkien, I saw the dichotomy of good and evil," David says. "We can't allow evil to stop us. We can't let roadblocks that crop up stop us from being about God's business. There were stumbles and turns and obstacles on Bilbo's journeys, but that didn't keep him from continuing on. Like him, we must continue our journey."

Reading *The Hobbit* changed David Copeland's life in a number of significant ways. The lessons and reminders from the book are still with him today; they permeate his consciousness as great books do for all of us.

Without a doubt, the most important book for Christians to read and study is the Bible. We should never replace reading other books with reading the "Book of the ages." Christians can benefit, though, from reading books other than the Bible—both classics and contemporary ones. From classic writers such as St. Augustine and Teresa of Avila to Janette Oke and Max Lucado today, readers have a wide choice of worthwhile books that will not only help them better identify with the basic eternal problems of human beings but will enrich their souls and lift their spirits.

BOOKS ADD TO OUR LEARNING

"For wisdom will enter your heart, and knowledge will be pleasant to your soul," said the writer of Proverbs (Prov. 2:10). He also admonished, "Let the wise listen and add to their learning" (Prov. 1:5).

Great books provide us wisdom and knowledge if we "listen" carefully to their meaning, ponder them, meditate on their great truths, and then make application to our lives. Even if the books are written for entertainment such as the Christian writer J. R. R. Tolkien said his were, we can be entertained as well as fed spiritually and guided by the timeless, universal principles we find in them.

The Apostle Paul provides a great example of the role of reading and books. He wrote to Timothy: "For I am already being poured out like a drink offering, and the time has come for my departure" (2 Tim. 4:6). As he awaited trial and death, what did he want? His books! His request to Timothy was, "When you come, bring the cloak that I left with Carpus at Troas, also the books, and above all the parchments" (2 Tim. 4:13 RSV).

THE INFLUENCE OF BOOKS

Devotional writer Oswald Chambers loved books. He wrote to a friend, "I do thank God for my books with every fiber of my being. Friends that are ever true and ever your own."

C. S. Lewis grew up in a home with books. He said in *Surprised by Joy* that they were everywhere including in the study, drawing room, cloakroom, and bedroom. He said, "Nothing was forbidden me. In the seemingly endless rainy afternoons I took volume after volume from the shelves." Lewis aptly wrote from his experience, "No book is really worth reading at the age of ten which is not equally (and often far more) worth reading at the age of fifty and beyond."

The great devotional writer Thomas à Kempis said, "If he shall not lose his reward who gives a cup of cold water to his thirsty neighbor, what will not be the reward of those who by putting good books into the hands of those neighbors, open to them the fountains of eternal life?"

Author Warren W. Wiersbe believes we should "read books that will help us serve the Lord better. . . . We must also read books that will help us build our lives and our homes—biographies of great Christians, the classics that have endured the test of time."

One of the 25 questions missionary Amy Carmichael had for potential missionaries to Dohnavur was, "Apart from the Bible, can you name three or four books which have been of vital help to you?" A voracious reader herself and author of 35 books, Amy realized the important role of books in a Christian servant's life.

Many people have come to a belief in Christ directly from reading a book, including David Livingstone, C. S. Lewis, and Charles Colson. The great Scottish missionary to Africa, David Livingstone, while reading Scottish clergyman-astronomer Thomas Dick's *Philosophy of a Future State,* became convinced that it was his duty and privilege to accept Christ's salvation.

The two authors who had their greatest influences on C. S. Lewis in his pilgrimage to become a Christian were George MacDonald and G. K. Chesterton. Then an atheist, Lewis loved MacDonald's adult fairy tale called *Phantastes* published in 1858. Chesterton, an English author, wrote over 100 books including the famous "Father Brown" detective stories. Lewis said of MacDonald and Chesterton, "A young man who wishes to remain a sound Atheist cannot be too careful of his reading. There are traps everywhere."

Tom Phillips, former president of the Raytheon Company, gave Charles Colson a copy of *Mere Christianity* by C. S. Lewis. Colson credits the book in his autobiography *Born Again* as the impetus for his conversion.

CLASSIC CHRISTIAN BOOKS

Christian readers today can choose from a vast number of classic Christian books that have inspired readers for years with their timeless truths and words. While it is impossible to list all of the classic Christian books available, some you may want to read include:

The Imitation of Christ by Thomas à Kempis
A Serious Call to a Devout and Holy Life by William Law
The Christian's Secret of a Happy Life by Hannah Whitall Smith
The Unselfishness of God by Hannah Whitall Smith
Foxe's Book of Martyrs by John Foxe
Abide in Christ by Andrew Murray
The Practice of the Presence of God by Brother Lawrence
Revelations of Divine Love by Julian of Norwich
Introduction to the Devout Life by Francis de Sales
On the Song of Songs by St. Bernard of Clairvaux
The Sacrament of the Present Moment by Jean-Pierre de Caussade
Pensées by Blaise Pascal
Table Talks by Martin Luther
Institutes of the Christian Religion by John Calvin
The Divine Conquest by A. W. Tozer
Each New Day by Corrie ten Boom
Evening by Evening by Charles H. Spurgeon
Morning by Morning by Charles H. Spurgeon
The Cost of Discipleship by Dietrich Bonhoeffer
How Should We Then Live? by Francis A. Schaeffer
My Utmost for His Highest by Oswald Chambers

Journals and Autobiographies

"One of the richest experiences you can have," says Warren W. Wiersbe in *Victorious Christians You Should Know*, "is reading the diaries and journals of great men and women in Christian history."

John Bunyan's *Grace Abounding to the Chief of Sinners* is his spiritual autobiography. It gives great insight into the life of the man who wrote one of the greatest books of all time, *Pilgrim's Progress*.

The great Scottish minister and missionary Robert Murray McCheyne drew inspiration from several journals: *The Letters of Samuel Rutherford*, *Memoirs of Henry Martyn*, and *The Life and Diary of David Brainerd*. Ironically, after his death his friend and fellow minister Andrew Bonar wrote *The Memoirs and Remains of Robert Murray McCheyne*, now itself a Christian classic. And after Bonar's death, his daughter edited *The Diary and Life of Andrew Bonar*, also now a classic!

For Richard J. Foster, author of *The Celebration of Discipline*, "no writing outside of the Bible has meant more to me than *Woolman's Journal*."

Other significant autobiographies and journals include:

The Life and Diary of David Brainerd
The Journal of George Fox
Journal of John Wesley
Surprised by Joy by C. S. Lewis
Jonathan Edwards' Journal
George Mueller's Journals (4 vols.)
Markings by Dag Hammarskjöld
Seven Storey Mountain by Thomas Merton
The Hiding Place by Corrie ten Boom
Just as I Am by Billy Graham

Biographies

Biographies of great Christians give us a glimpse into the lives of ordinary men and women who gave their lives to God and were used in a mighty way. They tell us about their prayer experiences, the role of Scripture in their lives, their stewardship, and their service to others.

Boswell's Life of Johnson by James Boswell is generally acclaimed to be one of the world's greatest biographies. A faithful Anglican, Samuel Johnson, who wrote the *Dictionary of the English Language*, was one of England's most pious writers. Other biographies about Christians that will inspire you are those written about Amy Carmichael, John Wesley,

Susanna Wesley, Fanny Crosby, Jonathan Edwards, David Livingstone, Charles Spurgeon, Catherine Booth, William Booth, Gladys Aylward, Mother Teresa, Sojourner Truth, Florence Nightingale, Harriet Tubman, George Mueller, Martin Luther, Corrie ten Boom, William Tyndale, Frederick Douglas, and Billy Graham. The list could go on and on.

Good biographical collections include:

Who's Who in Christian History, edited by J. D. Douglas and Philip W. Comfort

Twentieth-Century Dictionary of Christian Biography, edited by J. D. Douglas

More than Conquerors, edited by John D. Woodbridge

Ambassadors for Christ, edited by John D. Woodbridge

Great Leaders of the Christian Church, edited by John D. Woodbridge

Christian Novels

Christian novels can inspire and teach us through powerful plots, characters, and themes.

John Bunyan's *Pilgrim's Progress* has been called "the most popular Christian classic ever produced in the English-speaking world."

In His Steps, the best-selling novel published in 1897, continues to challenge readers today. The story by Charles Sheldon with characters challenged by their pastor to ask, "What would Jesus do?" inspired the recent WWJD movement.

Other great Christian novels include classics like *The Robe*, and *Ben-Hur*, romance novels by Grace Livingston Hill, and a wide variety of books written by contemporary Christian novelists.

Secular Novels

The truths of Christianity can also be communicated through the pages of secular novels.

J. R. R. Tolkien wrote *The Hobbit*; The Ring Trilogy: *Fellowship of the Ring*, *The Two Towers*, and *The Return of the King*; and *The Silmarillion.* C. S. Lewis's *Chronicles of Narnia* are classic stories. Tolkien and Lewis both wrote fantasy stories from a Christian perspective.

Madeleine L'Engle's books, including her award-winning fantasy *A Wrinkle in Time,* are modern-day classics.

Many American Christian writers have achieved fame as secular novelists. One of the most devoted to her faith was Flannery O'Connor who also wrote short stories. Her writings include *Flannery O'Connor: The Collected Works*; novels *Wise Blood* and *The Violent Bear It Away*; and short story collections *A Good Man Is Hard to Find* and *Everything That Rises Must Converge.*

Other examples of secular novels that can speak to Christian souls include:

Nikolai V. Gogol's *Dead Souls*

Fyodor Dostoyevsky's *Crime and Punishment* and *The Brothers Karamazov*

Aleksandr Solzhenitsyn's *One Day in the Life of Ivan Denisovich* and *The Gulag Archipelago*

Leo Tolstoy's short story collections and *War and Peace*

Jane Austen's *Pride and Prejudice* and other novels

Charles Dickens's *A Christmas Carol, The Life of Our Lord*, and others

Victor Hugo's *Les Miserables* and others

Drama and Poetry

The plays of William Shakespeare speak timeless truths about life, death, morality, and faith.

Many of the great poets throughout history were committed Christians, including Dante Alighieri, Geoffrey Chaucer, John Donne, John Milton, William Wordsworth, William Blake, Gerard Manley Hopkins, T. S. Eliot, Christina Rossetti, Robert Browning, and Elizabeth Browning. Their works can inspire and invigorate us.

INFLUENTIAL BOOKS FOR LEADERS OF THE PAST

Many great Christian leaders of the past gave much credit for their spiritual growth to books.

Teresa of Avila wrote that she was "given the *Confessions of Saint Augustine*, and I think the Lord must have ordained this, for I did not ask for the book nor had I ever seen it. . . . When I started to read the *Confessions*, I seemed to see myself in them."

John Wesley was most influenced by these devotional books: *The Imitation of Christ* by Thomas à Kempis, *Holy Living and Holy Dying* by Jeremy Taylor, and *A Serious Call to a Devout and Holy Life* by William Law.

Ann Judson, one of the first American missionaries, cited Hannah More's *Strictures on Female Education*, John Bunyan's *Pilgrim's Progress*, and Bellamy's *True Religion* as being influential in her spiritual development.

Lottie Moon, the great missionary to China, loved Thomas à Kempis's *Imitation of Christ*. It was one of the few books besides the Bible that she treasured.

Catherine Marshall, like millions of others who have read it, was greatly influenced by Hannah Whitall Smith's classic book *The Christian's Secret of a Happy Life*. Marshall wrote in her best-selling book *Beyond Our Selves* that she read Smith's book over and over. "Her emphasis was that the Christian life is the happiest of all lives. . . . She insisted that Christian joy could not be bought cheaply," Marshall wrote of Smith. Marshall went on to say that "there was no evading the total surrender of one's life and resources, no avoiding the giving up of doubt and the giving in to a costly obedience."

Jim Elliot, martyred missionary to Ecuador, read the diaries and biographies of great missionaries such as David Brainerd, Jonathan Goforth, and Hudson Taylor. He wanted to imitate their faith.

BOOKS THAT HAVE INFLUENCED PEOPLE TODAY

We asked several people, all avid, lifelong readers, to talk about books that have influenced their lives. We hope their insights will challenge you to consider some of their recommendations.

Calvin Miller, professor of preaching and ministries studies at Beeson Divinity School, Samford University, and himself prolific author, believes that Christian growth is greatly aided by reading classic Christian books. "Becoming Christlike demands years. It requires all the strength we have," he writes in his book *The Unchained Soul*. "The sources of this strength are easily identified: the indwelling Christ, the Bible, counselors, friends, and the voices of those devoted Christians who, across the ages, have fought battles similar to our own."

In *The Unchained Soul,* Miller writes about ten devotional books that have had a major impact on his life:

The Confessions of St. Augustine by St. Augustine
The Autobiography of Madame Guyon
The Practice of the Presence of God by Brother Lawrence
The Way of Perfection by Teresa of Avila
The Showings of Revelations by Julian of Norwich
Pilgrim's Progress by John Bunyan
The Cloud of Unknowing by Unknown Author
Selected Works of Bernard of Clairvaux
The Sacrament of the Present Moment by Jean-Pierre de Caussade
The Imitation of Christ by Thomas à Kempis

Rick Lance, executive director of the Alabama Baptist Convention and a voracious reader, recommends several books that have influenced his life. *Man's Search for Meaning* by Viktor Frankl "is one of my favorite books," he says, " because it reveals how one Holocaust survivor found meaning in the worst of life's circumstances. Following World War II, Viktor Frankl used his life experiences to help others face their own adversities."

His second choice is *Truman* by David McCullough. "Although I always admired President Harry S Truman, my appreciation for him was enhanced through my reading of this well-written biography. The common man who became the great man is the subject of this life story."

Lance also points to *Postmodern Pilgrims* by Leonard Sweet. "*Postmodernism* is a popular term used widely today in theological and cultural circles. Leonard Sweet's book is a very good explanation of the meaning and implications of postmodernism. His practical yet theological work was a tremendous help to me concerning the challenge of communicating the gospel in a postmodern world."

He highly recommends *Churchill on Leadership* by Steven Hayward. "I have been an admirer of Winston Churchill since my youth," he says, "and I have enjoyed reading about his interesting life. Steven Hayward has gone beyond a biography of Churchill to a detailed study of his leadership style."

Restoring Your Spiritual Passion by Gordon MacDonald has also influenced him. "MacDonald is an insightful writer, and his book on rediscovering your spiritual passion is a fine example of that giftedness. MacDonald is one author who can speak to both the heart and the head."

The last book he cites is *The Prayers of Peter Marshall* by Catherine Marshall. "Early in my ministry I read the sermons of Peter Marshall and his biography, *A Man Called Peter*. Later I discovered a compilation of prayers that serve to be a rich source of devotional support for daily living."

John Armistead, novelist, children's writer, religion writer, and minister, cites three books that have influenced him: Nikos Kazantzakis's *The Last Temptation of Christ*; William Temple's *Nature, Man and God*; and Reinhold Niebuhr's *The Nature and Destiny of Man*.

Dennis Hensley, a prolific author says, "The book that has had the greatest impact on my life is *Martin Eden* by Jack London. First, because it is the honest portrayal of a young writer's efforts to impact the world through his writings, and his eventual success at that. Secondly, however, because at the end of the novel, when Martin has achieved wealth, fame, prestige, honors, and influence, he stills lacks a sense of peace because he has no relationship with God. As a result, he sees the glories of the world as being shallow. . . . So he commits suicide. The story is poignant, emotionally powerful, and artistically brilliant."

"Among Christian writers, the works of C. S. Lewis have touched me, particularly *Mere Christianity*," Hensley says. "His logic, transparency, and wisdom stand the test of time."

Cecil Murphey, another prolific author, says, "If I had to pick one writer in recent years who has most influenced me it would have to be Henri Nouwen. My admiration for him began when I read his *Wounded Healer* in the early 1970s. Nouwen is the only writer I've read, and sometimes reread, that continues to push me toward growth," he says.

Murphey also mentions Philip Yancey ("not because he's always so insightful, but because he writes so beautifully") and Calvin Miller ("I especially like his earlier works"). He adds: "I'm currently reading *Ruthless Trust* by Brennan Manning, and it speaks to me where I am. I've just finished Robert Benson's *Living Prayer*. Benson tells stories and talks about liturgy. Sometimes I wonder where's he's going, and then he throws in a few paragraphs that make my eyes moisten. Somehow he connects with me.

"From time to time I go back and reread some of the older writers, such as Bishop John Riley, who wrote nearly 200 years ago. The only Christian book that I've read more than 10 times is *The Practice of the Presence of God* by Brother Lawrence. Every two or three years I feel drawn back to it. Another book I used to read until I loaned it to a friend who never returned it was *Letters by a Modern Mystic* by Frank Laubach.

"Along with prayer, reading is the most important aspect to my Christian growth. When I was in graduate school, I sensed the importance of reading and promised God and myself that I would read at least one book a week for the rest of my life. I've held to that commitment."

Murphey says that reading is an extremely important spiritual discipline to practice today. "It's important to be in church, to worship with others, and to serve in various capacities, but those are the outward commitments. Prayer and reading are the private, unseen parts of our commitment. We can fake our spirituality in service; but if we don't have that private life, it shows," he says. "I have learned so much from reading the insights and experiences of others through the years."

He says that reading fulfills a need to know more about God. "I do a lot of reading out of my search to know more about God, about myself, and about the world," he says. "I read out of my sense of need and ask, Where am I now? What kind of books will satisfy my immediate hunger?"

He also credits secular books. "I read secular writers because no one has an exclusive contract on God's secrets. Two examples. A couple of years ago the book *Tuesdays with Morrie* taught me an invaluable lesson that we learn to live only when we face dying. A decade ago, Alice Miller's *Drama of the Gifted Child*, helped unlock parts of myself I didn't know existed."

Angie Cooper, a missions leader in her church and community and a lifelong reader, delights in reading contemporary as well as classic writers. One of her favorite books is *What Happens When Women Pray* by Evelyn Christenson. "I sensed a feeling of awesomeness when I first read the book, the idea that women's prayers can be so powerful. We come from a background where men are always praying," Angie says. "I was glad that someone finally dispelled the myth that it is men's prayers that are making things happen."

Of *My Utmost for His Highest* by Oswald Chambers, she says, "Every time I pick it up it is exactly what I need for that day. It is so relevant." A recent book that has shaped Angie's thinking is *Women Who Loved God* by Elizabeth George. "I've always been fascinated by women of the Bible who walked with God. Now I can walk daily with them and joyfully discover new spiritual truths."

The Unselfishness of God by Hannah Whitall Smith is another favorite. "This book was moving to me because Hannah didn't know what she was searching for," Angie explains. "She was seeking the will of God, a void in her life. The book tells of her discovery of the unselfishness of God."

Author Bruce Evensen, professor of journalism at DePaul University, says, "If I had to take only one book on a desert island, other than the Bible, it would probably be something from Kierkegaard or Lewis. There is much to admire in Kierkegaard's existential Christianity because he captures so beautifully the Suffering Servant and our need to receive Him through a 'leap of faith.' Lewis and his *Mere Christianity,* articulated over the BBC during World War II, encouraged that generation and remains an everlasting blessing. Malcolm Muggeridge's *Christ and the Media* and *Chronicles of Wasted Time* are particularly splendid for students of the media. He crashes through skepticism late in life and is particularly helpful for intellectuals who hesitate at the water's edge.

Evensen also recommends reading poetry. "Among the poets, I would urge readers to consider Milton, Auden, and Elliot," he says.

"Elliot's 'The Love Song of J. Alfred Prufrock' anticipates the postmodern impulse to nihilism and self-absorption."

Evensen encourages Christians to do any research that will bring them nearer to an appreciation of Who Christ is. "The more you study the spiritual life of previous generations, the more you will appreciate how similar our struggles and ultimately our triumphs can be as we share them with those who have come before and will come after," he says.

June Matthews, a freelance writer, read *Experiencing God* through a study at her church and was deeply affected by it. "Since the *Experiencing God* course had such an impact on my life, I am particularly fond of anything written by Henry Blackaby. I recently read *The Ways of God* that he coauthored with Roy Edgemon and got excited all over again thinking about how God reveals Himself to us in a million ways every day. Most of the time, we don't notice; but when we sit up and pay attention, wow! He's really busy!" June says. "Blackaby brings that simple message home in all of his work that I've read and it's taught me to be more mindful of God's presence in my life."

A favorite book that first comes to mind for Carolyn Barrett, a homemaker and mother, is *A Guide to Prayer* published by the Upper Room and edited by Reuben P. Job and Norman Shawchuck. "A great devotional book, it is a book of guided prayers and meditations. It includes readings from classics such as Teresa of Avila and Henri Nouwen. It also provides a place for journaling," she says.

She also mentions *Disciplines of the Beautiful Woman* by Anne Ortlund. "This book influenced me a lot because it helped to focus me, made me think of my goals, and helped me organize."

God Calling and *God at Eventide*, edited by A. J. Russell, are powerful devotional books. "These two are devotional books written by two women that decide that they will listen to God and do what He says and keep a record of what happens," she says.

Of *The Radiance of the Inner Splendor* by Lloyd John Ogilvie (current chaplain of the US Senate), Carolyn says, "This book helped me to know that eternity begins now. It helped me to value myself. It is about the fruits of the Spirit that change us."

Carolyn also enjoyed *The Christ of the Mount* by E. Stanley Jones. "This book about the sayings of Jesus on the Sermon on the Mount helped me to understand the words of Jesus for the first time," she says. "It got me excited about His message."

Jan White, Christian bookstore owner and avid reader, often recommends books for the customers in her store. "As for classic Christian books, I would recommend *Celebration of Discipline* by Richard Foster. Oswald Chambers's devotional *My Utmost for His Highest*, and Andrew Murray's *Absolute Surrender* are heavy-hitters for deep thinkers and may be a bit overwhelming for new Christians. Classics would also include *Hinds Feet on High Places* by Hannah Hurnard, *The Christian's Secret of a Happy Life* by Hannah Whitall Smith, and *In His Steps* by Charles Sheldon. I would also recommend allegories like *Pilgrim's Progress* and the *Chronicles of Narnia*."

Angela Payne, nurse and author says that Catherine Marshall has always been one of her favorite female writers. She recommends *Adventures in Prayer*, *Beyond Our Selves*, and *Something More*. "I frequently pull any or all of these from my bookshelf," Angela says.

Elisabeth Elliot is another favorite of Angela's. "*The Glad Surrender* is excellent," she says. "There is no fluff or gush about her writing . . . just the truth."

"My very favorite male writer is Ken Gire. *Windows of the Soul* is always nearby. It is moving and profound and beyond words," Angela says. "His *The Reflective Life* is also outstanding."

Although her life is incredibly busy, lawyer and mother Ree Glaze tries to find time for reading. "Two books have been both influential and inspirational to me. The first is *The Power of the Praying Wife* by Stormie Omartian," she says. "The other is *Grace for the Moment*, a daily devotional derived from various works of Max Lucado."

OTHER AVENUES OF PERSONAL STUDY

Books are not the only tools to enrich your personal study time. Other effective tools include books on tape and reading material on the Internet. Many Christians also rely on conferences and retreats, seminars, and other special events to increase their understanding of the Christian life.

It seems fitting that this chapter on personal study ends on the important role that God has on a writer's life. Nikolai V. Gogol (1809–1852), Russian novelist of *Dead Souls*, was a deeply committed Christian. He believed that God had given him his literary talent to teach the Russian people the righteous way of living in an unrighteous world. He once said, "The word must be treated honestly. It is the highest gift of God to man. . . . All the gifts of God are given to us so that we may serve our fellows."

PERSONAL QUESTIONS ABOUT PERSONAL STUDY

- Am I familiar with great Christian devotional classics? Do I frequently read them?
- Do I read Christian fiction?
- Am I reading the classic secular novels written by Christians?
- Do I read biographies and journals of great Christians?
- Is God calling me to go on a private retreat to do some intense personal study and reading?

MAKING PERSONAL STUDY PART OF YOUR LIFE

- Determine at the beginning of each year to study a Christian classic.
- Commit to read a book a month or even a book a week.
- Incorporate the reading of Christian books into your devotional time each day.
- Read Christian classics meditatively. Study the works of people like Augustine, Thomas à Kempis, John of the Cross, Oswald Chambers, Evelyn Underhill, etc.
- Read for inspiration; then share with others inspiring books that have touched your life.
- Read biographies and journals of great Christian men and women.
- Don't be intimidated about your lack of reading; determine to read and internalize what you do read.
- Start a book club with others in which you read a Christian classic each month.
- Enroll in a book study course through your church where you study a Christian book.

LIFE APPLICATION VERSE

"For wisdom will enter your heart, and knowledge will be pleasant to your soul" (Prov. 2:10).

PRAYER

Lord, give me a desire to read only those books that have meaning and value. Help me choose my books carefully because what I read will influence me always. Thank You for being my help as I strive to deepen my love for You and others through my reading. In the name of Jesus. Amen.

8
Guidance

"When we really rely on the Holy Spirit, He will guide us. We from our side must fulfill one important condition: obedience."—Corrie ten Boom (1892–1983), World War II concentration camp survivor, world evangelist, and author

"Show me your ways, O Lord; teach me your paths, guide me in your truth" (Psalm 25:4).

Ashley Fisher and other single adults sat down for their afterchurch prayer group and began to mention individuals and their various needs. Someone immediately brought up the name of Bobby Britt. Pastor at First Baptist Church of Trussville, Alabama, Britt had undergone dialysis for 5 years and was in need of a kidney transplant.

As the group prayed, Ashley felt a sudden and strong tug on her heart. "All of a sudden I felt God telling me that I should go forward and be tested as a possible donor," she remembers.

Once the prayer ended, Ashley asked more about Britt's condition and later called him and his wife. They were astonished to hear such an offer from a woman Britt had never met.

The process to donate her kidney began, and, during the entire time, Ashley says it was clear that God was guiding her steps. He sent words of comfort and signs of reassurance to her all along the way.

On the day she had preliminary blood work done, she flipped open a magazine to a story about an athletic trainer donating a kidney to someone; as she waited to have her blood drawn, she kept seeing her last name Fisher on different items; the man who drew her blood also had the name of Fisher. On the way home, she read a bumper sticker that said, "Don't take all your organs to heaven—be an organ donor"; at home she turned on the television to see a story about a man waiting for a kidney donor for his daughter.

"I felt like these were signs from God telling me I was in the right place," she says. "I was whispering a prayer under my breath and I softly said, "OK, God, I understand."

The process to donate the kidney was not always easy because she had to deal with people's confusion about what she was doing. "But I told them that God was leading me to do this," she says.

After an unexpected delay of several months, the transplant was successfully performed. Both Ashley and Britt came through the surgery well.

Like Ashley, all Christians should seek God's guidance, not just for the big decisions like donating a kidney, but in every aspect of our lives. God will let us know what He wants us to do, but we must seek it and trust in His revelations to us.

Seeking God's guidance and then following it in obedience, however, is not always easy. We tend to want to follow our own directions, seek out our own dreams, and create our own paths. Following God's guidance is another critical Christian discipline we need to develop.

WHAT DOES THE BIBLE SAY?

Many verses in the Bible speak about guidance. From the prophet Isaiah to the nation of Israel in exile we read, "And your ears will hear a word behind you saying, 'This is the way, walk in it'"(Isa. 30:21). Later he said, "The Lord will guide you always; he will satisfy your needs in a sun-scorched land and will strengthen your frame. You will be like a well-watered garden, like a spring whose waters never fail" (Isa. 58:11).

Instructions about guidance, now for individual followers of Christ and His Church, continue in the New Testament. The Gospel of John teaches that if we are Christians, we will follow God's guidance. "He who belongs to God hears what God says. The reason you do not hear is that you do not belong to God" (John 8:47).

WHY DO WE NEED GOD'S GUIDANCE?

When we acknowledge that we need God's guidance with the details of our everyday lives—marriage, children, parents, career, hobbies, church activities, school, friendships—we hand over the reins to our Master. We say, "You know what's best in all of these situations, no matter how insignificant they may seem to me. I'm asking You to guide me and show me what I should do."

When the adversities of life come our way, we also need to seek God's guidance. Whatever it is, grief, relationship problems, an ailing parent, a rebellious child, bad habits, loneliness, depression, physical problems, or financial setbacks, God is present. His comfort, strength, and guidance help us through situations we otherwise could not successfully survive on our own.

The Psalms reassure us that God's guidance is always available and that it is always correct. "I will instruct you and teach you in the way you should go; I will counsel you and watch over you," the writer says in Psalm 32:8.

The popular nineteenth-century minister Henry Ward Beecher (1813–1887) said, "The strength and happiness of a man consists in finding out the way in which God is going and going in that way too."

Our life truly depends on seeking God's guidance and then following it in obedience.

SEEKING GUIDANCE

Through the centuries committed Christian men and women have given us insight into how to seek guidance.

Hannah Whitall Smith (1832–1911), in her classic *The Christian's Secret of a Happy Life*, offered four ways to find guidance: "through the Scriptures, through providential circumstances, through the convictions of our own higher judgment, and through the inward impressions of the Holy Spirit on our minds."

Evangelist R. A. Torrey (1856–1928) wrote in *How to Succeed in the Christian Life* that there are five points in seeking guidance. First, "recognize your ignorance and inability to guide your own life." Second, "surrender your will to God." Third, "have definite prayer time." Fourth, "have confident expectation that God will guide you." Fifth, "follow step-by-step as He guides."

Missionary Amy Carmichael (1867–1951) combed the Book of Acts for principles of guidance. She discovered it came "through circumstances, through careful thought, through the general feeling which followed prayer and fasting, by an impelling sense of duty, or a word from the Lord."

In her book *This Day Is the Lord's*, Corrie ten Boom (1892–1983) wrote that God speaks "through His Word, the Bible; in the talks we have with Him when praying; through other people; and through that which is happening around us. If we take time to listen, we shall hear Him."

In his *Experiencing God* book and course, author Henry Blackaby says that "God speaks by the Holy Spirit through the Bible, prayer, circumstances, the church, and other Christians to reveal Himself, His purposes, and His ways."

The Holy Spirit

Jesus told His disciples that the Holy Spirit "will guide you into all the truth" (John 16:13). Author Catherine Marshall (1914–1983) asserted, "We have to ask the Spirit to lead us; then by an act of will place our life situations and our future in His hands."

Corrie ten Boom had similar wisdom when she said, "He will guide us by His Spirit if we ask Him to do so, if we are submissive to Him and refuse to be led by our own wishes."

Bible Study

Scripture guides us to truth. As Corrie ten Boom said, "God also uses our daily Bible reading to show us the way we have to take, the decision we have to make. God has promised to honor the daily use of His Word in our lives."

When Deborah Guinn graduated from high school, her desire was to move far away from her hometown of Fayetteville, Arkansas. "I watched jealously as most of my friends went away to school and came back with great stories of new friends and activities while I still lived at home; attended the University of Arkansas in the same town I grew up in; and had the same old, dull life I'd always had. Boy, was I bitter!" she remembers.

One day during her quiet time, Deborah's Bible "fell open" to Habakkuk 2:3. She read, "For the vision is yet for the appointed time; it hastens toward the goal, and it will not fail. Though it tarries, wait for it; for it certainly will come, it will not delay."

"It was then that I realized that God knew my needs and my desires and was not going to make me 'suffer' through the 'bad' times," she recalls. "But I had to wait for His timing, not mine."

Deborah knows now that God's timing and plan was perfect. He led her down the right path to an ideal job as a director of an outdoor camp for children.

The Word of God is replete with assurances that God's plans are always good for us. "For I know the plans I have for you," declares the Lord, "plans to prosper you and not to harm you, plans to give you hope and a future. Then you will call upon me and come and pray to me, and I will listen to you. You will seek me and find me when you seek me with all your heart" (Jer. 29:11–13).

We should always evaluate our thoughts and decisions against biblical truth by searching the Scriptures. "'As the heavens are higher than the earth, so are my ways higher than your ways and my thoughts than your thoughts,'" declares the prophet in Isaiah 55: 9. The Bible helps us know if our desires are in line with God's.

English minister Charles Spurgeon in *Morning by Morning* summed up the Bible's role well. "Be assured that thy God will be thy counsellor and friend; He shall guide thee; He will direct all thy ways. . . . Happy are we to have God's Word always to guide us!"

Meditation

God often speaks in quiet ways. Listen for that voice as you meditate on the Scriptures or sit in silent praise.

Shirley Lashley heard God's quiet voice whisper to her one day to serve Him as a missionary. A retired nurse, Shirley had never entertained the idea. She was naturally puzzled, yet kept her options open; after all, she says, this was God speaking to her. Not much later, Shirley heard God's quiet voice again; this time it whispered the word, "Israel." She would never have chosen that as her destination and had no idea how to go to Israel as a missionary; she didn't even have a missions agency to send her.

In obedience to that voice, though, Shirley sought God's guidance, and He opened up remarkable doors for her. Just two months after hearing God's directions (and after selling everything she owned),

Shirley flew to Israel to teach elementary school children at the Jerusalem Christian School.

Prayer

Through prayer, we open up ourselves to God and ask Him to do His will in our lives. Like Jesus did, we need to seek daily guidance from the heavenly Father. Through prayer we get new insights, thoughts, or a call to action.

Abolitionist Sojourner Truth (c. 1797–1883) asked for God's guidance throughout her life. When she escaped from slavery in 1827, she asked God for direction. When He gave her the thought to leave before daylight, she said, "Thank You, God, for that thought!" She then asked God, "Where, and to whom, shall I go?" and He gave her the name of a man who then directed her to a couple who employed her.

She told Harriet Beecher Stowe (1811–1896), author of the great classic *Uncle Tom's Cabin*, how she happened to change her name (Belle, short for Isabella, which her former master had given her) after she was a free woman. "I went to the Lord and asked Him to give me a new name." She remembered Psalm 39:12. "Hear my prayer, O Lord, and give ear unto my cry . . . for I am a stranger with thee, and a sojourner, as all my fathers were." She thought of another Bible verse, John 8:32. "And ye shall know the truth, and the truth shall make you free."

When she needed help from people, she would ask God, "Oh, God, make the people hear me—don't let them turn me off, without hearing and helping me." She thanked God when people helped her. "God only could have made such people hear me; and he did it in answer to my prayers."

Fasting

Many Christians fast because they want concentrated time to ask God for guidance. Among the people in American history who dedicated much time to fasting was the missionary David Brainerd (1718–1747).

In his diary, he poured out his desire to sacrifice himself for God. He spoke often of his fasting to prepare himself for his work with the Native American Indians in New England. In 1742 he wrote: "Monday, April 19. I set apart this day for fasting and prayer to God for His grace; especially to prepare me for the work of the ministry, to give me divine aid and direction. . . . Monday, June 14. I set apart this day for secret fasting and prayer, to intreat God to direct and bless me with regard to the great work I have in view, of preaching the gospel. . . . Wednesday, June 30. Spent this day alone in the woods, in fasting and prayer."

Journaling

Nurse Florence Nightingale (1820–1910) was one of many people through the ages who have sought guidance through journaling. She recorded: "On February 7th, 1837, God spoke to me and called me to His service." She had asked God for guidance and prayed continually for a word from Him. Florence was certain that it came on that day.

On May 12, 1850, she wrote, "Today I am thirty—the age Christ began His mission. . . . Now Lord, let me think only of Thy Will what Thou willest me to do—Oh Lord Thy Will, Thy Will."

On May 21, 1850, she wrote, "Let me only accomplish the Will of God. Let me not desire great things for myself."

On her 32nd birthday, she wrote, "I am glad to have lived, though it has been a life which, except as the necessary preparation for another, few would accept. I hope now that I have come into possession of myself."

Finally, in early 1853, after seeking God's guidance for 16 years, her calling was apparent. She was chosen to manage a hospital for women in London. God led her the next year to Crimea to a hospital where she supervised the care of thousands of British soldiers. They looked upon her as a "ministering angel" as she made her solitary rounds with her little lamp in her hand. Honored by the English people for her tireless work in the Crimean War, she remained humble. At her death she requested to be buried in the family grave instead of Westminster Abbey. Her tombstone bears the simple inscription: F. N. Born 1820. Died 1910.

Worship

Many people feel the pull of God on their lives during worship services. Musical presentations, sermons, Scripture readings, prayer,

Communion, confession—all of these parts of the worship experience God can use to guide and direct His followers.

Individuals have accepted Christ; missionaries have felt called to service; people have felt convicted of sin; church members have felt God's call to action . . . all during worship services.

Other people

God also uses other people as instruments of guidance. God may use a spouse, a child, a parent, a close friend, or a total stranger to guide us in a certain situations.

When best-selling novelist Terri Blackstock asked for God's guidance, the direction came through a person. "When I made the decision to quit writing secular romance novels and give my career to the Lord, I had a lot of concern about how to get started in the Christian market," she remembers. "Because I'm a creative person and don't have a business mind, I've always worked with an agent who could take care of the business aspect of marketing my books. I was looking for a Christian literary agent, one that had the same vision I had for my books."

Terri spoke to one agent who agreed to represent her, but she had a feeling of uneasiness about her decision. "I wasn't sure this was the one God wanted for me," she says. "So my husband, Ken, sat down and prayed with me, and we asked the Lord to show me clearly if this was the right person, and if it wasn't, to send the right person. We asked the Lord to act quickly on this, since I was ready to start submitting my work to publishers."

A couple of hours later, Terri and Ken were in separate cars listening to the same Christian radio show. The guest was a man named Greg Johnson, who turned out to be a literary agent. "Ken felt an overwhelming sense that this was the answer to our prayer, so he pulled his car over at a pay phone, and called the station to get Greg's number," Terri says. "When the interview was over, he called Greg in Colorado and told him about me, and asked him if he would be interested in representing me."

Terri was initially upset at Ken's impulsiveness, but then called and talked to Greg. "The moment I had Greg on the phone, I knew that this was God's answer to our prayer of that morning," she says. "I was amazed at the caliber of authors they represented. I realized that God hadn't sent me just any agency. He had sent me the best, and I was honored to be in such company." She has since written many Christian novels and now teams up with Beverly LaHaye to write novels.

God not only uses other people but also their written words to guide and direct us. Countless books have inspired and guided people over the years (see chap. 7).

Circumstances

Corrie ten Boom once said, "Our circumstances often are God's answers to our prayers. We pray for patience, and God sends us someone demanding the utmost of our strength. We pray for selflessness, and God gives us opportunities to get rid of our self."

We see evidences of that truth in our daily lives. A phone call from a friend comes at just the right time; a move brings you to the right neighborhood where you can make a difference for Christ; a stranger becomes a person you can witness to. God guides us through all the circumstances of our lives; we simply must be aware of Him working in those situations.

Franki Putman's dream after graduating from college was to be a freelance writer, but she was unsuccessful. She went back to school, got a master's degree in education, and began teaching. When proration struck, however, she lost her job and found herself in another job that she couldn't tolerate.

"I didn't like this job, and I would often talk to God and ask Him how I could have possibly gotten so far off track," she remembers. Soon opportunities arose, however, and she took a new job that involved writing. One job led to another; by the time she was pregnant with her first child, she felt like giving freelance writing a try.

"Even when I thought nothing was working out and my job was the pits, God had a plan. If I hadn't taken that job I so strongly disliked, it would not have led to the next job and then the next which eventually led to my dream, mom/freelance writer," she says. "I just believe that God has a plan for us; and even when things in our lives seem confusing or out of control, it's all part of the plan. If we keep praying, keep listening, and keep trusting, He will not let us down."

There are no coincidences. "In all things God works for the good of those who love him, who have been called according to his purpose," Paul declared in Romans 8:28. God uses circumstances to create results.

Author Oswald Chambers said we must open up to God in the midst of our circumstances. "Every time circumstances press in on you, say, 'Speak, Lord,' and make time to listen," he said.

Dreams

God can use any tools He desires to get our attention, even our dreams.

Author Robert Morgan tells John Claypool's story of a young woman who went to China as a missionary teacher. She started the journey with a deep sense of God's calling, but during the long boat trip over the Pacific Ocean she began having doubts. Overcome by worries, one night she dropped off to sleep and had a powerful dream.

"It was as if she were standing in the middle of the ocean all by herself with nothing but a two-by-four supporting her at the surface of the water," Morgan wrote. "A voice said to her, 'Start walking to China.' She answered back, 'But I can't. I'm not able to walk on water. If I leave this secure standing place, I will drown.' But the voice insisted. 'I said walk. Start walking toward China.' With fear and trembling, but in obedience, she lifted her foot and put it forward, and just at that moment that it was touching the surface of the water, another two-by-four appeared out of the depth. Every step she took was met by support emerging from the deep. She woke with a new sense of confidence."

THE NEXT STEP: OBEDIENCE

Jesus said, "Whoever has my commands and obeys them, he is the one who loves me" (John 14:21). The beloved hymn "Wherever He Leads I'll Go" reiterates His words.

The discipline of guidance is closely tied to the discipline of obedience. As God guides us, the proper response is obedience.

Jesus was always obedient. He always submitted to His Father's will. His obedience led him to the Cross. "And being found in appearance as a man, he humbled himself and became obedient to death—even death on a cross" (Phil. 2:8).

And in 1 Samuel 15:22 we read, "Does the Lord delight in burnt offerings and sacrifices as much as in obeying the voice of the Lord? To obey is better than sacrifice."

Bible commentator Matthew Henry (1662–1714) expounded on that Scripture by saying, "Humble, sincere, and conscientious obedience to the will of God is more pleasing and acceptable to him than all burnt offerings and sacrifices. . . . Nothing is so provoking to God as disobedience, setting up our wills in competition with his."

When best-selling author Henry Blackaby was called to pastor churches in Canada, he went in obedience, but had no idea how far the move would take him.

"Our time in Canada took an enormous amount of obedience. But I am totally convinced that I would not have written *Experiencing God* had I not been in that place at that time and stayed for the long haul," he says.

Because of Gladys Aylward's (1902–1970) obedience, God used her in a mighty way. While a parlor maid, she was converted and felt called to be a missionary to China. Rejected by the China Inland Mission because of her lack of educational qualifications, she set out alone in 1932 on an incredible journey from London to Yangcheng. Upon her arrival, she worked at an inn with another missionary and then became an itinerant evangelist.

In 1940 the Japanese invaded Shanghai Province where she served. One hundred children were housed at a compound near the enemy lines. Since their lives were in danger, Gladys agreed to guide them from Yangcheng over the mountains to Sian where Madame Chiang Kai-shek had an orphanage. Biographer Alan Burgess wrote of the historic and hazardous journey, "Keeping a hundred children out of sight and earshot of enemy soldiers who were often in the region was the most strenuous aspect of the long journey."

God protected them and met all of their needs. After more than five weeks of traveling through mountainous terrain, they reached their destination safely, except for Gladys who collapsed, near death. After her recovery, she stayed in the city working with refugees. Later her poor health led her back to England. Years later she went back to the Orient and opened an orphanage in Taiwan. The film *The Inn of the Sixth Happiness*, starring Ingrid Bergman, recounts the heroic story of this humble housemaid who, in obedience to God's call, went to China and was used by God to accomplish an incredible feat.

Obedience involves obeying God in all areas of our lives—service, prayer, Bible study, stewardship, and worship. It means obeying God at home, at work, wherever we are.

Henry Blackaby believes that much of God's activity is in the workplace among unbelievers. He says, "God's concern is that He finds somebody to obey Him in the workplace, someone who will believe that He will honor his or her faithfulness in unusual ways. All through Scripture God asks His children to remember that He put them where He wants them to be, and that He wants to accomplish something through them."

PERSONAL QUESTIONS ABOUT GUIDANCE AND OBEDIENCE

• Do I seek God's guidance daily?
• Do I obey God immediately and joyfully?
• Do I sometimes feel unsure of God's calling in my life? Can I trust Him to reveal to me the direction I should go?
• Before saying yes or no to a ministry opportunity, do I ask God's guidance first?
• When has God used Bible study to guide me?
• When has He used prayer or meditation?
• When has He used a worship service?
• When has He used other people or circumstances?
• Have I recently obeyed a clear call from God?

MAKING GUIDANCE AND OBEDIENCE PART OF YOUR LIFE

• Consider setting aside a time for evaluation a half a day three or four times a year to pray for God's direction in your life,

• Record in your journal how God has guided you.
• Ask God's guidance each day about your activities, how you respond to others, how you witness, etc.
• Ask God to guide you through the trials and stresses of your life.
• Copy and frame one of the Bible verses from this chapter and put it somewhere in your home so you will be reminded daily of God's guidance.
• Ask God to help you obey His commands in the Scriptures.
• Ask God to help you obey Him by getting involved in a ministry to which He is calling you.
• Thank someone who by his or her obedience to God has influenced your life.

LIFE APPLICATION VERSE

"Trust in the Lord with all your heart and lean not on your own understanding; in all your ways acknowledge him, and he will make your paths straight" (Prov. 3:5).

PRAYER

Thank You, God, for Your guidance. Help me to be disciplined to seek Your daily guidance in all areas of my life. Then help me follow You in obedience. Amen.

9

SIMPLICITY

"He who has God lacks nothing; God alone suffices."—Teresa of Avila (1515–1582), patron saint of Spain

"For in Him we live and move and have our being" (Acts 17:28).

One of the greatest women in Christian history, Teresa of Avila believed in primitive simplicity. Her life was characterized by austerity. Her own tiny room had no furniture. She had no cover except a piece of sackcloth. Yet, in this seemingly rigid atmosphere she wrote her masterpieces and carried on a wide correspondence. Her five major books, including *The Interior Castle* and *The Way of Perfection,* place her among the greatest of Christian writers.

The only woman in history that the Catholic Church gave the title of Doctor of the Church, she founded the Discalced (Barefoot) Carmelites, a reformed order which spread to several continents. She founded 16 nunneries and 14 convents. In her many travels she always requested the most humble quarters for herself.

Her nuns' habits were of coarse brown serge; their veils had no pleats or folds. They wore their hair short, slept on straw, ate no meat, and were confined to their cloister.

Teresa's life was focused completely on God. In *The Way of Perfection*, she wrote to her fellow sisters about surrendering themselves to God, "Cease to be anxious for yourselves, for He bears your anxiety, and will bear it always. It is as though a servant had gone into service and were anxious to please his master in everything."

Simplicity, sincerity, quiet intensity of purpose, humility, and spiritual power were her trademarks. It seems fitting that at her death these lines she had written on a slip of paper were found:

He who has God lacks nothing;
God alone suffices.

Brother Lawrence (1611–1691) also understood and embraced simplicity. He lived it. He learned how to focus on Jesus even amid the clutter going on around him.

Born in Lorraine, France, as Nicholas Herman, at the age of 18 he served in the Thirty Years' War. Wounded, he returned home, haunted by memories of the savage fighting. One winter day he found himself staring at a bare tree stripped of its leaves. He suddenly realized that like the tree that would grow leaves again, his life would be fruitful again.

Someone wrote of him, "It was then that he received an insight into the providence and power of God." When he was around 50 years of age, he joined the Discalced Carmelite monastery in Paris as a lay brother. Given the name of Brother Lawrence of the Resurrection, he was assigned to the kitchen where he spent much of the next 30 years. He died in the monastery.

The first several years in the kitchen were ones of discouragement. He eventually, though, reached the state where he found himself experiencing God's presence constantly in his life.

He learned the secret of letting nothing come between himself and God. He kept his eyes fixed on God not only in times of worship but also as he washed pots and pans. "The time of business," he said, "does not with me differ from the time of prayer, and in the noise and clatter of my kitchen, while several persons are at the same time calling for different things, I possess God in as great tranquillity as if I were upon my knees at the blessed sacrament." When people asked him about his joy, he told them about practicing the presence of God in life's little duties, thinking about God all the time.

He left no major writings, only a few spiritual notes and letters. In fact, he destroyed much of what he did write because he thought it worthless. Soon after his death, his superior, the abbot of Beaufort, put together the conversations he had with Brother Lawrence and 15 letters into a book called *The Practice of the Presence of God*. This slim little book has influenced generations of Protestants and Catholics alike and continues to do so today.

The Bible speaks often of the redeeming nature of simplicity. In leading a life focused on the simple truths as Teresa of Avila and Brother Lawrence did, and not getting caught up in the busy cycle of life and all of its stresses, we lead a life more in tune with what God wants. When our hearts and minds and lifestyles are set on Christ, we have our priorities aligned properly.

Matthew 6:33 clarifies these priorities. "But seek first his kingdom and his righteousness, and all these things will be given to you as well."

The Bible admonishes us, "Since, then, you have been raised with Christ, set your hearts on things above" (Col. 3:1–2) and "Love the Lord your God with all your heart and with all your soul and with all your mind and with all your strength" (Mark 12:30).

Jesus taught His followers to keep away from worrisome thinking and to focus instead on what's truly important in life. "So I tell you, don't worry about everyday life—whether you have enough food, drink, and clothes. Doesn't life consist of more than food and clothing? Look at the birds. They don't need to plant or harvest or put food in barns because your heavenly Father feeds them. And you are far more valuable to him than they are" (in Matt. 6:25–26 NLT).

Other biblical writings remind us of "the simplicity that is in Christ" (2 Cor. 11:3 KJV) and advise us to "delight yourself in the Lord and he will give you the desires of your heart" (Psalm 37:4).

The Old Testament reminds us that when we seek after God, we find what truly matters. "You will seek me and find me when you seek me with all your heart" (Jer. 29:12–13). We need only seek God; it's a simple, but very profound, truth.

Simplicity, then, should be one of those spiritual disciplines to which we aspire.

WHAT IS SIMPLICITY?

Simplicity, in the spiritual sense, is having a center to our lives, an inner attitude, and a steadying focus. We focus on God, first and above all else, and clear out clutter so we can center on Him.

In the very busy and often complicated world we live in, a loving relationship with God is a safe and constant refuge. Amid all of the responsibilities of day-to-day life, we can find contentment in God's loving arms.

St. Augustine (354–430) put it this way, "Thou has made us for Thyself, and the heart of man is restless until it finds its rest in Thee."

When we analyze our busy lives and try to accomplish everything on our mile-long to-do list, it is encouraging to know that in God we can find simplicity and rest. R. A. Torrey understood this when he said, "There is more joy in Jesus in twenty-four hours than there is in the world in 365 days. I have tried them both."

Simplicity, then, is the way to escape the busyness and restlessness of this world and connect with Christ in a day-to-day way. It clarifies our lives and keeps us in touch with the things that truly matter.

Rebecca Jordan, author of *At Home in My Heart*, strives for simplicity in her daily life. She knows that it's the only way to keep truly focused on Christ.

"A quote I wrote and will continue to use is 'Simplicity is not a fad-i-tude, but an attitude of the heart.' It is finding that 'one thing that is needful,' that Jesus talked about with Martha," Rebecca says. "Simplicity is rooted in a relationship and is tied to balance. Anne Ortlund once said we were to cut through the clutter and concentrate on the important. And I think that's what simplicity is in the spiritual sense as well as the physical sense. Simplicity is paring down the heart to the real essential—Christ Himself—where He is at home in our hearts."

In her book *A Place Called Home*, Harriet Crosby defined simplicity. "Simplicity is not just another interior design option. It is also one of the great expressions of Christian faith. Simplicity is devoting our lives to one thing and one thing only—to loving the Lord our God with our whole being and our neighbors as ourselves."

WHY WE NEED SIMPLICITY

Mother and freelance writer Karen Holcomb remembers reading all of Laura Ingalls Wilder's "Little House" books as a child. She and her two sisters received the book as gifts from her parents and spent many years enjoying the stories of Laura, Ma, Pa, and the entire Ingalls family; she relished the moments when she'd travel in her imagination to life in the Kansas log cabin. Their life was very alluring because it was simple.

"Even now, I cling to the images of the simple life in those books," Karen says. "Pa cut down trees for the log house while Ma washed the girls' dresses, drying them in the sun. Things have changed and my life does not reflect this simplicity."

Karen appreciated and yearns for the simplicity found in Wilder's books. Wilder herself understood the need for simplicity as it relates to a Christian's life. In fact, any woman living today in the twenty-first century could easily have uttered her statements on simplicity.

"We are all busy, but what are we living for anyway, and why is the world so beautiful if not for us?" she asked. "Let's not make such a habit of hurry and work that when we leave this world, we will feel compelled to hurry through the spaces of the universe using our wings for feather dusters to clean away the star dust."

In modern society many people are seeking the simplicity that Laura Ingalls Wilder wrote about a century ago and the simplicity that Karen yearns for today. Many books have been written about the topic; people are seeking peace and calm in the midst of life's difficulties; both Christians and nonbelievers are trying to find real meaning by getting back to the simple things of life.

For Christians, though, the reason for attaining simplicity is not so simple (pardon the pun). It's vital if we are to have an honest, clear, open relationship with God. And we cannot work forward from that relationship and serve others if we do not simplify to some degree.

"Our lives are just as full, if not more so, as non-Christians," says Rebecca Jordan. "It is difficult to see other people as Jesus did when all we see is our own stress and stretched out lifestyles. In a spiritual sense, how can you minister out of an empty tank?"

When we live in simple faith and with the right priorities, we reflect to others the Truth we know. "Simplicity exhibits a childlike trust that says my Father is in control, even though I struggle just like you do," Rebecca says. "I believe the simplistic attitudes Jesus gives us (loving freely, forgiving completely, accepting totally, trusting daily, etc.) say to other women, 'Hey! there is something to this Christianity.'"

Simplicity is also important if we are to forge ahead in other areas of spiritual discipline. How can we find the time for prayer if our lives are hectic and harried? How can we devote ourselves properly to worship if we are consumed with worry and details? How can we spend any time at all in reflective Bible study if we are too busy making appointments and meeting deadlines?

Simplicity can, simply put, make us more effective Christians.

EXAMPLES OF SIMPLICITY

Jesus is the ultimate example of leading a life of simplicity. He focused solely on one thing, fulfilling the will of His Father.

Jesus' disciples followed His example when they left everything and followed Him. When He first called them, He instructed them, "Follow me and I will make you fish for people" (Mark 1:17 NRSV). Their response was a simple acceptance of Who He was; they acted in obedience: "At once they left their nets and followed him" (Mark 1: 18).

In the years and centuries since, Christians have followed their example and lived lives of simplicity in obedience to Jesus' calling on their lives.

The great English poet Christina Rossetti (1830–1894) also led a life of simplicity, completely focused on Christ. She lived much of her life in poor health, with little money, and no home of her own. Yet, her Christian faith enabled her to have an amazing serenity of purpose and live a quiet, humble life.

Christina, her sister, and two brothers learned the Bible from their devout mother. Their father, a poet and political refugee from Italy, was professor of Italian at Oxford and a Dante scholar (he could quote the entire *Divine Comedy* by heart!). Growing up in various dingy homes in London, Christina was surrounded by the creativity of artists and writers. Her first poems were published when she was 12. When her book *Goblin Market and Other Poems* was published in 1862, she was proclaimed an original poet.

She worked in the home of her brother William for 40 years. In 1871 she was stricken with Graves' disease. Accepting her affliction with courage and resignation, she lived 23 more years mainly preoccupied with her devotional writing. She wrote over 900 poems in English and 60 in Italian.

Dante and the Bible with commentaries were her constant reading companions. Whenever her health permitted, she did church work. Some of her poems have become beautiful Christmas carols; "In the Bleak Mid-Winter" and "Love Came Down at Christmas" are favorite ones.

The timid, modest Christina never boasted of herself or her creative gifts. Even when she was dying, she asked her church to pray for her but to not mention her name.

Making Christ the center of her life, she displayed her creative focus in one of her beautiful hymns, "None Other Lamb."

None other Lamb, none other name,
None other hope in heaven or earth or sea,
None other hiding-place from guilt and shame,
None beside Thee.

My faith burns low, my hope burns low;
Only my heart's desire cries out in me
By the deep thunder of its want and woe,
Cries out to Thee.

Lord, Thou art Life, though I be dead;
Love's fire Thou art, however cold I be:
Nor heav'n have I, nor place to lay my head,
Nor home, but Thee.

Today Christians continue to struggle with simplicity. We might reason that missionaries who serve in remote places find simplicity more easily. They too, however, struggle with making their lives simpler and more at peace.

Cheryl Nance and her family serve in South Korea with the International Mission Board; when they're on stateside assignment, they often have people jokingly say, "I guess you need to go back to the field so you can rest." Cheryl says that statement is far from the truth.

Their lives are packed with activities and action from the work she does developing missions materials, to the Sunday School class and Bible study she teaches, to the support she gives her husband, to her sons' soccer and piano lessons, to helping with homework. She searches for some semblance of simplicity in her life.

"Our lives are just like yours," she says. "We have everything you have here except it is in a foreign setting. Our life is very busy."

PRACTICING SIMPLICITY TODAY

We often use the busyness of modern life as an excuse for lack of simplicity in our lives. We need to remember that Jesus was busy, but He focused on the Father and His purpose in life. We know from reading the Book of Acts that the Apostle Paul was busy, but he led a focused life. Like Jesus and Paul, we can keep our hearts centered on Christ.

How, though, do we do it? How do we keep our priorities on Christ instead of on the busy, complicated matters of everyday living?

Simplicity is not necessarily giving up all the trappings of modern life, but it can mean scaling back and asking, "What is truly important to me?"

In *How to Make People Really Feel Loved*, Charlie Shedd gives guidelines for simplifying life:

- Drop useless goals.
- Don't try to do it all yourself.
- Live one day at a time.
- Enjoy what you're doing right now while you're doing it.
- Develop a hobby.
- If it is impossible to slow your world down, slow yourself down.
- Adopt the perfect pattern, which is Christ. Study Him as He lives a life in quiet confidence.

Contemporary authors Bruce Bickel and Stan Jantz (better known simply as Bruce and Stan) say that seeing God in the big things of life is easy. The challenge is in seeing God in the small, simple, even mundane activities of life. "We need a divine perspective about the details of life. We mustn't overlook God in the small stuff," they say. "When we realize God is in the ordinary, our daily grind suddenly has meaning and purpose. The household chores become an opportunity to express love and care for other members of the household. A walk to the mailbox brings a chance to greet the neighbor who may be in desperate need of an encouraging word. The day at work presents the challenge of giving wholehearted effort which will be pleasing to God. Live your life with an overwhelming sense that God is present in the details all around you."

Seeing God in the small stuff of life is an excellent way to see what's truly important. Madeleine L'Engle, popular author of *A Wrinkle in Time* and other books, also appreciates this practice. She says we must appreciate the small joys and the seemingly insignificant moments. "When we forget the obvious, the little joys, the meals together, the birthday celebrations, the weeping together in time of pain, the wonder of the sunset or the daffodil peeping through the snow, we become less human," she says.

Author Anne Morrow Lindbergh found much of her inspiration beside the seashore; it even taught her about simplicity. "One cannot collect all the beautiful shells on the beach," she says. "One can collect only a few, and they are more beautiful if they are few."

Rebecca Jordan finds simplicity in the symbols of simplicity she places in and around her home. "These symbols are reminders to keep my heart's attitudes centered on Christ. I have a candy jar to remember to make my home a forgiving place, and the hall tree to hang my burdens on Christ. The hammock is a place where I meet the Lord repeatedly—as is my desk in my home. In other words, it is a physical place that helps me visualize a peaceful, serene attitude—and a heart centered on Him."

Another excellent way to cultivate simplicity in your otherwise overcrowded, complicated life is to develop a life mission statement.

Sandy Brooks, author and director of CWFI (Christian Writers Fellowship International), encourages each Christian to develop a mission statement for his or her life and believes doing so will create a simplicity of purpose. A mission statement is a written statement of a goal, a goal for work or for life in general.

"Forming a mission statement simplifies your life because it helps you stay focused, and makes you more effective and productive on the day-to-day journey of fulfilling your assignment," Sandy says. "It also helps you to prioritize your life so that the assignment is more likely to be fulfilled."

Sandy developed her mission statement early in her writing career, when she got stuck on a magazine article she was trying to complete. After several days she set it aside and decided to pray. "I prayed, 'Lord, if You don't want this article published, that's fine, but I don't want to spend anymore time on it if You can't use it for kingdom purposes," she remembers. "The next morning during my quiet time the phrase, 'That They May Know Him,' floated through my mind. After recording it in my prayer journal, I meditated on what the Lord was saying to me. In a few moments, it dawned on me. That's what was wrong with my article. It focused more on me and my experience than it did on His work in my life and circumstances. He was to be the center of my work, not me."

She went on to print out a piece of paper with her statement, That They May Know Him, written on it. "I framed it, and hung it in my office. Every day, I'm reminded that He is to be the focus of every writing assignment. Not me, not my writing ability, but Him!"

Rebecca Jordan has also developed a mission statement for her career and life. It has helped her keep things in perspective, she says. "Everyone's mission statement and goals are different," Rebecca explains. "But that's part of simplicity—finding your chosen niche and appointed tasks in this life, whether as a mom, teacher, wife, board member, or president."

SIMPLICITY VERSUS MATERIAL POSSESSIONS

Our image of simplicity is usually one of pioneer days when men and women had very few material possessions or one of missionaries living overseas in a tiny hut with few items of luxury. Is this what simplicity involves? Does simplicity necessarily mean a turning away from material possessions or wealth?

Simplicity can mean living with few luxuries, but it doesn't necessarily have to. Wealthy men or women can live lives of simplicity, if their priorities are straight and their inner lives are filled with contentment and calm.

The primary objective is to discover which is of a higher priority in your life. Does having a luxury car or expensive home interfere with your ability to love God simply and completely? If there is a struggle between the two, perhaps you need to change some things.

"If material possessions clutter your heart and steal your affections, by all means get rid of some. Periodically, give some things away anyway—it is good for you. I try to get rid of something each time I buy something," Rebecca Jordan says. "And I am a collectaholic, so this is a challenge."

Rebecca says she knows many wealthy people who are marvelous stewards of their possessions; these men and women practice simplicity in the midst of wealth. The key, she says, is to determine who owns whom. Do you own the possessions or do the possessions own you?

THE REWARDS OF SIMPLICITY

If simplicity is so important, why do so few Christians practice it? Anne Morrow Lindbergh said, "Today, more of us in America than anywhere else in the world have the luxury of choice between simplicity and complication of life. And for the most part we, who could choose simplicity, choose complication." Lindbergh wrote this in 1955, but how true it is still today!

Why don't we see the joy and the rewards that come from a life of simplicity? Why don't we realize that a close, connected relationship with God is possible only when the other priorities have been relegated to second place?

To be truly disciplined as a Christian, we need to rediscover these rewards. We must realize what author Oswald Chambers said. "Simplicity is the secret of seeing things clearly. . . . When the natural power of vision is devoted to the Holy Spirit, it becomes the power of perceiving God's will and the whole life is kept in simplicity."

Perhaps the greatest argument for simplicity in a Christian's life comes from the example we receive from the Christmas story. In realizing how simple, and yet profound, God's gift was to us, we can get back to the simple joys and beauties of life.

In her book *Soul Searching*, Debra Klingsporn reminds us that God came to us in a very real, tangible, human way. The sacred was cloaked in the simple; the holy was hidden in the ordinary.

"If God only made his presence known in the momentous, how barren our lives would be. Instead, there are snowfalls and rain showers, waking and sleeping, as we live a succession of ordinary days," she writes. "Into our ordinary world we are given this hidden God, one who comes to us as a baby born amid hay and barnyard smells to a nondescript couple of an ordinary night. Into the ordinary came the extraordinary. The birth of a Savior. And our lives will never be the same."

PERSONAL QUESTIONS ABOUT SIMPLICITY

- Have I ever considered the role of simplicity in my life?
- What keeps my life from being one of simplicity?
- How can I practice simplicity in my own life?
- Do I need to clean out the clutter in my life so I can center on God?
- What are some practical steps I can take to simplify my life?

MAKING SIMPLICITY PART OF YOUR LIFE

- Find a Bible that highlights the words of Jesus. Read them so you can focus on the sayings of Jesus.
- Slow down and enjoy God's creation, the beauty around you: the sunrises and sunsets, the stars, the singing of the birds, the opening of a rose.
- Begin the day by reciting Psalm 118:24. "This is the day the Lord has made; let us rejoice and be glad in it."
- Take breaks throughout the day to focus on God and simply enjoy Him.
- Spend an entire day focusing on God.
- Do simple activities that you may neglect in the busyness of your life: go on a picnic, read aloud favorite poems, hold your spouse's hand as you walk through a park.

- Say no to a lot of activities that clutter your life.
- Take a calming break by drinking a cup of herbal tea, taking a walk in a garden, or sitting on your porch.
- As your life becomes more complicated, strive to keep things simple.
- Do not envy others who have more material things than you do.
- Look around your home and see what you really don't need. Pray that God will reveal to you who may need these things, and give them away.
- Declutter your home by giving clothes and furniture to a shelter.
- Organize your household by designating a place for everything.
- Before you buy something else, give something away.
- Take magazines to physicians' offices and books to a library or literacy ministry.
- Eliminate or limit the television you watch for a week. Replace the time you watch television with Bible reading, prayer, or the reading of Christian literature.

LIFE APPLICATION VERSE

"But seek first his kingdom and his righteousness, and all these things will be given to you as well" (Matt. 6:33).

PRAYER

Help me to focus on Jesus. Reveal to me how to remove the clutter from my life so I can prioritize the most important things. In the busyness of my life, help me to keep focused on Christ. In the name of Jesus. Amen.

10

STEWARDSHIP

"Christ says, 'Give me All. I don't want so much of your time and so much of your money and so much of your work: I want You.'"—C. S. Lewis (1898–1963), English author

"As he looked up, Jesus saw the rich putting their gifts into the temple treasury. He also saw a poor widow put in two very small copper coins. 'I tell you the truth,' he said, 'This poor widow has put in more than all the others. All these people gave their gifts out of their wealth; but she out of her poverty put in all she had to live on'" (Luke 21:1–4).

She never received more than $.50 a week, but she managed to save the remarkable sum of $345.83, which she gave to missions. Her gift was the first one offered to the American Board of Commissioners for Foreign Missions.

Like the widow in the Bible, Sally Thomas (1769–1813), a servant girl in Cornish, New Hampshire, gave all she had. A member of the Congregational Church in Cornish, Sally worked for 23 years for the Daniel Chase family and died at the age of 44. Little is known of Sally, but her gravestone inscription speaks volumes: "By the labor of her hands she had acquired property amounting to about $500; which by her last will, excepting a few small legacies, she gave for the spread and support of the Gospel."

Sally gave out of her poverty as many through the ages have; countless others have given out of their wealth. One such person was a young man who only lived to be 26 but still inspires us today.

When news of the death of William Borden (1887–1913) was cabled from Cairo, Egypt, in April 1913, newspapers throughout America carried an account of the young man who had given so much of himself and his wealth to the world.

Born into a family of privilege (his father made his money in silver mining), William became a Christian at the age of 7 under the preaching of the famed Chicago minister R. A. Torrey. He attended Yale

University where he boldly witnessed for Christ. He chose two Bible verses as his mottoes for college: "Wherewithal shall a young man cleanse his way? by taking heed thereto according to thy word. . . . Thy word have I hid in mine heart that I might not sin against thee" (Psalm 119:9,11 KJV).

While at Yale, William was active in the Student Volunteer Movement and committed himself to be a missionary to the Muslims of China. At this time, he also began the Yale Hope Mission, a Skid Row rescue mission. While at Princeton Seminary, he taught a Sunday School class in an African Methodist Episcopal Church and gave away $70,000 to several Christian causes (his father had died while he was in college). He also became a director of the Moody Bible Institute and wrote its doctrinal charter.

After his graduation from Princeton Seminary in 1912, he was ordained at the Moody Church in Chicago. The newspapers covered the event because it seemed strange to many that a young millionaire would choose a missionary career.

William, who refused to own a car because he thought it was poor stewardship, wrote his last will only weeks before he sailed to Cairo on December 17, 1912, to share the gospel with Muslims. Ministering diligently for only three months, he became ill on Easter 1913 and died on April 9 of cerebral meningitis. At his death, his almost $1 million was given to such ministries as the China Inland Mission, National Bible Institute, and Moody Bible Institute.

Although his life was a short one, in life and in death he left a legacy of true devotion to Christ and to the things that matter most. Samuel Zwemer, noted missionary to the Muslims in China, said at his funeral, "Borden won the victory over an environment of wealth. He felt that life consisted not in 'the abundance of things that a man possesseth.'"

Christians today share in the legacy of both Sally Thomas and William Borden. We are commanded to give, whether it is out of our poverty or our wealth, in response to the most amazing gift that God has given to us through His Son.

Author Larry Burkett, the founder of Christian Financial Concepts, says that our entire lives must be in stewardship to God. "God expects us to have an exclusive commitment to Him and to the lordship of Christ. Jesus said, 'Anyone who does not carry his cross and follow me cannot be my disciple.' Commitment of the whole person is the basis of good stewardship."

We all "must account for every thought, every word, every deed, every penny, every neglected opportunity, every talent, every breath, every look, every step," wrote Robert J. Hastings in *My Money and God.* "The ideal steward can withhold nothing, waste nothing, dissipate nothing, clutch nothing to his breast," he said.

We must give our whole person—not just our money but also our possessions, gifts/talents, time, physical body, mind, service, and attitudes—to the will and toward the work of God. Only then are we truly practicing the discipline of Christian stewardship.

WHAT IS STEWARDSHIP?

Wanda Lee, executive director of Woman's Missionary Union® (WMU®), describes stewardship in this way: "God, as the Creator of all of life, has entrusted us with everything we are and have—our body, mind, soul, talents, time, and possessions. The Greek word for entrusted is translated 'to deliver to one something to keep, use, take care of, manage.' God has graciously given each of us many wonderful gifts and abilities. He desires that we use those in service for Him.

"At some point in our lives, we begin to recognize all the wonderful things God has provided for us, and then our desire grows to use those gifts appropriately," she says.

We are to give ourselves to God. It's that simple. We should use our time, gifts and abilities, money, and possessions to serve God. Our stewardship of faith dictates how we give in all of these various areas of our lives.

Giving is a priority to a Christian. In obedience, we put God first in our lives. In return, we trust Him to provide for our daily needs.

Larry Burkett says that it all comes down to the idea of ownership. We must decide who owns our lives. Do we own them? Or does God?

"Who owns your 'things'? What about the house you live in, the car you drive, your 'toys' such as golf clubs? What about your personal abilities and future earning potential? Who's the owner of all these things?" he asks. "If your answer is, 'I am,' you have a stewardship problem. The Bible tells us that God owns all things."

Stewardship is not just a duty. It is also a joy and a source of blessings. The more we give of our time, talents, and resources, the more spiritual blessings will be ours.

The Bible teaches us: "It is more blessed to give than to receive" (Acts 20:35); "You will be enriched in every way for your great generosity" (2 Cor. 9:11 NRSV); and "God loves a cheerful giver" (2 Cor. 9:7). Stewardship builds up the church in practical ways and serves others through a variety of ministries; it also blesses us more than we could ever expect.

Love for God is directly connected to giving back to Him.

THE BIBLE AND GIVING

The Bible is full of instruction about stewardship. In fact, almost two-thirds of the parables of Jesus deal with finances. He was very clear on the topic—Christians are expected to be good stewards of everything they have.

Here is just a small sampling of what the Scriptures teach us about stewardship:

"Honor the Lord with your wealth, with the firstfruits of all your crops" (Prov. 3:9).

"Why spend money on what is not bread, and your labor on what does not satisfy?" (Isa. 55:2).

"The lover of money will not be satisfied with money; nor the lover of wealth, with gain" (Eccl. 5:10 NRSV).

"The earth is the Lord's, and everything in it" (Psalm 24:1).

"But store up for yourselves treasures in heaven, where moth and rust do not destroy, and where thieves do not break in and steal. For where your treasure is, there your heart will be also" (Matt. 6:20).

"Strive first for the kingdom of God and his righteousness, and all these things will be given to you as well" (Matt. 6:33 NRSV).

"The righteous are generous and keep giving" (Psalm 37:21 NRSV).

"Give, and it will be given to you. A good measure, pressed down, shaken together, running over, will be put into your lap; for the measure you give will be the measure you get back" (Luke 6:38 NRSV).

"So then, men ought to regard us as servants of Christ and as those entrusted with the secret things of God. Now it is required that those who have been given a trust must prove faithful" (1 Cor. 4:1–2).

Jesus said, "From everyone who has been given much, much will be demanded" (Luke 12:48).

The familiar story of Jesus feeding the 5,000 with five loaves of bread and two fish (John 6:5–13) teaches us a great lesson about stewardship. This miraculous work showed His disciples, and shows us, how much He can do with a little when we place it in His hands. Jesus has the power to take our resources, however limited, and multiply them for His ministry when we give them to Him.

God can work wonders with our gifts; He cannot use our gifts, though, if we are holding on to them selfishly. We must release them from our tight grasp and give them over to Him.

THE SPIRIT OF GIVING

Sarah Jackson Shelton remembers the day that her 7-year-old son heard a presentation about missions at their church. A woman told of the needs she and others had working in hospitals and on the missions field with sick children.

Upon arriving home, Sarah's son ran to his room and began sorting through a pile of stuffed animals. He announced to his mother, "She can use my animals to tell the sick children that Jesus loves them. Maybe one of mine will go as far away as Chile!"

Sarah says that her son's response made an indelible impression on her own attitude about giving. "His heart had been forever marked with a perception that, even as a child, he had something worthy to give. He was learning how to have a giver's heart," she says.

Stewardship can be reduced to an act of ritual and repetition, something we do only out of a sense of duty. To be meaningful in a spiritual way, though, we must practice it with an attitude of love and generosity; we must develop a giver's heart, just as Sarah's young son did.

According to Brian Kluth, the president of the Christian Stewardship Association, an attitude of joy will flow naturally from a heart that has its priorities straight. "It is God's grace and love that will give you the ability to give and share according to what He's given you," Brian says. "Your Christian giving is to be more delight than drudgery, more privilege than pressure, and more anticipation than anxiety."

The Bible puts it this way, "If I give all I possess to the poor and surrender my body to the flames, but have not love, I gain nothing" (1 Cor. 13:3).

The spirit of giving should also be one of understanding why we are doing it in the first place. It must be one of thankfulness for God's greatest gift to us.

Judy Bates, the founder of Bargainomics, a Christian organization devoted to proper stewardship, says that she must always keep this in mind. "In 1 Corinthians 6:20 the Apostle Paul reminds us, 'You are not your own; you were bought with a price.' This is one of the Scriptures on which Bargainomics is based," she says. "Being a good steward begins by recognizing that as one who has been redeemed by the blood of the Lamb, all I have, all I am, my past, my present, my future belongs to Him."

What flows from this understanding and thankfulness is a changed set of priorities. "Jesus said to 'seek ye first the kingdom . . . and all these things shall be added unto you' (Matt. 6:33 KJV). He didn't say, 'Seek ye second and some of these things,'" Judy says. "When God is first, our priorities are straight. When He is first, everything else follows in proper order. When He is first, all these things are added to His children."

STEWARDSHIP IS ALL-ENCOMPASSING

When we think of stewardship, we automatically think of giving money. Stewardship, though, involves much more than just money, possessions, time, and talents. We truly are to be stewards of our entire lives.

"Good stewardship is all-encompassing—time, money, attitude, your entire being—must be fully surrendered to and fully aware of the accountability you have before Jesus Christ," Judy says.

STEWARDSHIP OF MONEY AND POSSESSIONS

If we seriously examine our attitudes toward our money and possessions in light of biblical teaching, we will be generous, because that is what God expects.

Evangelist Billy Graham says, "God has given us two hands—one to receive with and the other to give with. We are not cisterns made for hoarding; we are channels made for sharing."

"Make all you can, save all you can, give all you can," advised Methodist founder John Wesley.

Author William Law wrote, "We would doubt the spiritual depth of a person who claims to lead the Christian life without prayer. But to ignore our own use of time and money is as foolish as ignoring prayer."

Individuals throughout history as well as people today provide us with much inspiration on how we can be generous with our money and possessions.

C. T. Studd. When C. T. Studd (1862–1931) received his father's inheritance of $150,000, he gave it all away after reading what Jesus said to the rich young ruler (Luke 18:18–23). Son of a wealthy plantation owner, C. T. was educated at Cambridge where he won fame as a cricket player. After his conversion at one of evangelist D. L. Moody's revivals at Cambridge, he devoted himself to missionary work. He and six friends he recruited became known as the Cambridge Seven. They laid the foundation of the Student Volunteer Movement with its purpose of recruiting college students as foreign missionaries.

In 1885 they arrived in China and worked with Hudson Taylor's China Inland Mission. When his father died, C. T. gave away his fortune. On January 13, 1887, he wrote out nine checks to various Christian organizations such as the Salvation Army, Moody Bible Institute, and George Mueller's orphanages.

Returning to England because of poor health, he then traveled to America inspiring many college students. He went to southern India in 1900 where for 6 years he served as a pastor. Poor health again led him to give up this work; but 1910 found him in central Africa where he established the Heart of Africa Mission. Completely spent for the Lord, he died in Africa.

C. T. Studd inspires us today to ask questions of ourselves: What is the purpose of our wealth? Even if our resources are limited, how can we give to God? How can we devote our pocketbooks to God's glory?

Our money can be used for great things, according to the writer of Hebrews. "And do not forget to do good and to share with others, for with such sacrifices God is pleased" (Heb. 13:16).

C. T. Studd's story also convicts us on another level. If we had great wealth, would we use it for similar things? Would we give it back to God? Or—be honest—would we use it simply for our own pleasure? In 1 Timothy 6:10 we read, "For the love of money is a root of all kinds of evil."

Money is amoral. It can be used for good or evil, depending on the motive of those spending it. What is your motive?

Missionary leader A. B. Simpson (1844–1919) said, "We must also lengthen the cords of our liberality. The Lord is asking for our wealth to spread His gospel. We to whom this gospel has been such a blessing are especially called to take it as our trust for Him and send it everywhere. . . . When I think of the opportunities of using money for God, I could almost envy the men who own successful businesses."

A. B. Simpson would have loved to meet R. G. LeTourneau and Truett Cathy. As businessmen, their lives offer great illustrations of the Christian stewardship of wealth.

R. G. LeTourneau. Born in Vermont, R. G. LeTourneau (1888–1969) was raised in a Christian home but found himself going down the wrong path at the age of 16. That pivotal year in his life he attended a series of revival meetings, and after one of the meetings was converted. He went on to build a successful business in Stockton, California. Then he suffered many hardships, including a broken neck, an almost deadly bout of influenza, and bankruptcy. Then through the death of his infant son God spoke to him about putting God first in his life ("Strive first for the kingdom of God and his righteousness, and all these things will be given to you as well" [Matt. 6:33 NRSV]) instead of worldly pursuits.

LeTourneau and his wife became involved in the Christian and Missionary Alliance Church and took up a challenge to be God's servants. God began using him to help shape North America through the mid-1900s. He is credited with inventing and perfecting nearly every type of heavy earth-moving machinery today. He supplied nearly 70 percent of the earth-moving machinery during World War II. With his amazing fortune, he began early on giving away money until he gave away 90 percent of his money. His famous quote still challenges us today: "The question is not how much of my money I give to God, but rather how much of God's money I keep for myself."

LeTourneau built a plant in Longview, Texas, and established LeTourneau College there. His life, called a working man's success story by many, showed what God can do through someone completely surrendered to Him.

Truett Cathy. Beginning with a tiny restaurant in the Atlanta suburb of Hapeville in 1946, Truett Cathy now leads the Chick-fil-A organization, one of the largest privately held restaurant chains and the second largest fast-food chicken restaurant company in the nation.

A devout Baptist, Truett Cathy is an entrepreneur who is a wise steward. Since 1973, his company has awarded restaurant employees more than $15 million in $1,000 educational scholarships. In 1984, he created at Berry College in Rome, Georgia, the $24,000 co-op WinShape Centre Scholarship Program. Today, the center includes a camp and homes which have foster care programs.

The closed-on-Sunday policy has not hurt Chick-fil-A; it now has 1,000 restaurants in 34 states and Washington, D. C. Maybe that can be attributed to the company's corporate purpose: "To glorify God by being a faithful steward of all that is entrusted to us. To have a positive influence on all who come in contact with Chick-fil-A."

In addition to money, we can also generously give material possessions. What do you own that can be used for God's glory?

Can you use your car to deliver meals to homebound members of your community or to transport neighborhood children to church? Can you give your used car to a charitable organization? Can you use your home to host a Bible study or to house visiting missionaries? Can you donate investments or a piece of land to your church or a Christian charitable organization? Can you clean out your closets and give your clothes to the needy?

The Bible encourages us to give. "If we have all we need and see one of our own people in need, we must have pity on that person, or else we cannot say we love God. Children, you show love for others by truly helping them, and not merely by talking about it" (1 John 3: 17–18 CEV).

STEWARDSHIP OF TIME

Not only can we be wise stewards of our money and material possessions, but we can also be wise stewards of our time. God wants to own our schedule! He wants us to use our seconds, minutes, hours, and days in ways that glorify Him. This means that we will use our time in meaningful pursuits such as prayer, Bible study, worship, and service.

When Stuart Calvert began her life as a pastor's wife, she quickly filled her schedule with a variety of activities. She joined the choir, visited shut-ins, taught adult Sunday School, led a youth group, visited hospitals, and led missions groups. "When I was not going somewhere, I was preparing for all the doing," she remembers.

She soon discovered, though, that something had to change. God could not work through her effectively unless she made some changes.

"First, I took a long look at self. Buried beneath what I assumed to be expectations of so many people, I found that I did not know who I was," she says. "Then I turned loose of some activities. The choir went first. Someone was waiting and willing to teach the adult Sunday School class. I concentrated on loving the young people and on developing my ability to work with them." Stuart found that her gift was in working with the youth of her church, but she discovered this only after devoting the necessary time to them.

In his book *Divine Conquest,* A. W. Tozer (1897–1963) said, "The man who would know God must give time to Him. He must count no time wasted which is spent in the cultivation of His acquaintance." Tozer's life certainly reflected that belief. The completely self-taught pastor (he had no formal education) became a deep Christian thinker and writer. He gave God much of his time. He wrote 40 books, one of which (*The Pursuit of God*), sold almost 1 million copies. He never owned an automobile and gave away most of his money to the needy. His tombstone bore the simple words: A. W. Tozer—A Man of God.

The Bible gives clear instructions about how we should spend our time. "Be very careful, then, how you live—not as unwise but as wise, making the most of every opportunity" (Eph. 5:16).

Jeremy Taylor (1613–1667), one of the greatest preachers of all time, wrote about the stewardship of time in his classic book *Holy Living*. He included 19 guidelines for using time wisely. They include such advice as "when you awaken, accustom yourself to think first upon God; and at night, let Him close your eyes" and "Fill hours of insomnia with prayer, since you have no requirements on your time then."

Stewardship of our time involves efficiently using our time for worthwhile pursuits. It means investing our time on earth, our work and leisure, wisely in service to God and others, for truly, our life is fleeting.

Playwright Thornton Wilder's character Emily in *Our Town* expressed her sentiments about time so well. "It goes so fast. We don't have time to look at one another. . . . Do human beings ever realize life while they live it—every, every minute?"

STEWARDSHIP OF GIFTS AND TALENTS

"You must begin to discover the gifts God gave to you, and then you must open them up and use them," said Corrie ten Boom, "that others can be blessed through you."

Christians are equipped with a variety of talents and spiritual gifts. Since God gives them, He expects us to use them for His glory. How, then, can you be a better steward of your gifts and talents? What gifts and talents can you dedicate to God?

Some can sing beautifully; others work well with children; some can teach or write; others can cook for the needy or grieving; others can quilt or crochet; some can manage money; some can organize; others can paint or draw; some can build houses for the poor; others can provide testimonies; others can comfort and encourage. Where do you fit in?

Businesswoman Carolyn Achterhof found her gift. A lay speaker, she also is a greeter for her church. Each Sunday she is the first person guests or members see when they walk into the church. "The greeter sets the tone for the church," Carolyn says. "I feel that being a greeter is one of my gifts, a gift of encouragement. I do what I do because I love people. Greeting people with a smile, a hug, an encouraging word is a way to show them that I love them. I feel God speaks through me. I may never know the extent of how He is using me to touch people, but I feel God is working through me.

"As the oldest child in the family, I was always the leader. I grew up in a small town where everyone knew everyone. I was always the one who would speak to (greet) strangers. I have always said that if smiles cause wrinkles, then I'd rather have happy wrinkles. I love to smile and greet people with a friendly smile. So many times you never know how much a welcome, a smile, an encouraging word can help a person. I believe that God uses us in ways that we are not aware of. I believe also that if you love God, you should use your gift.

"One Sunday morning a young career woman who has two children and a demanding career walked into our church. I greeted her with a hug as I usually do. The following Sunday she told me she wanted me to know that she had experienced a horrible week and that the only good thing about her whole week was the hug that I had given her that Sunday morning a week ago. I feel very blessed that God is using my gift to reach people."

STEWARDSHIP OF BODY

Another important element of a life of stewardship is stewardship of our physical bodies. Our bodies are a gift from God, and we are expected to treat them accordingly.

The psalmist so eloquently stated that we are "fearfully and wonderfully made" (Psalm 139:14). The Apostle Paul reminded us that we must respect our bodies. "Do you not know that your body is a temple of the Holy Spirit, who is in you, whom you have received from God? You are not your own. You were bought with a price. Therefore, honor God with your body" (1 Cor. 6:19).

When we think about what the Bible says about our bodies, it is really quite awesome. Our lives (and, therefore, our physical bodies) are extremely valuable. Each individual is precious; each person belongs ultimately to God; and God sacrificed His only Son for each one of us.

If our bodies belong to God, how then should we treat them? Should we go about our lives with no concern for our physical well-being? The answer is clear: we definitely should not!

We must take every effort to take care of our bodies. We must eat properly, protect our bodies from disease, exercise regularly, and abstain from harmful activities.

In doing so, we are giving a gift back to the God Who already owns us. We are honoring Him in our stewardship of our bodies. We then can join with Paul in saying that our "whole spirit, soul, and body be kept blameless" (1 Thess. 5:23).

STEWARDSHIP OF MIND

Jesus said, "Love the Lord your God with all your heart and with all your soul and with all your mind and with all your strength. The second is this: 'Love your neighbor as yourself.' There is no commandment greater than these" (Mark 12:30–31). Since Jesus commanded us to love God with all of our mind, it is a sin not to be a wise steward of our minds.

In *How Now Shall We Live?* author Charles Colson says that loving God with our mind means "understanding God's ordinances for all of creation, for the natural world, for societies, for businesses, for schools, for the government, for science, for the arts."

Henry Blamires, a student of C. S. Lewis, in his book *The Christian Mind: How Should a Christian Mind Think?* said, "There is no room in Christendom for a culture of the spirit which neglects the mind."

Charles Colson agrees with Blamires. Colson says sadly that many Christians have shunned intellectual pursuits and "have not developed a distinctively Christian perspective on all of life."

Colson says in *How Now Shall We Live?* that for him "developing a Christian mind is a rewarding and enriching act of discipleship." He says that after his conversion he felt his "mind born again, along with my spirit." Subjects such as history and science took on a new meaning for him because he saw them as "explorations of God's truth." He said, "It was as if a searchlight were shone into a cave, exposing the dark holes and crevices." Colson's insight brings to remembrance the words of the Apostle Paul when he said, "So that they may have the full riches of complete understanding in order that they may know the mystery of God, namely, Christ, in whom are hidden all the treasures of wisdom and knowledge" (Col. 2:2–3).

May we follow Colson's example and be proper stewards of our minds by exploring God's truths in the Bible as well as areas such as history, art, science, and literature. Then we will be intellectually able to, as Colson says, "defend God's truth."

SACRIFICIAL GIVING

We find evidence of true stewardship in sacrificial giving. We do not give what's easy for us to give; we make a sacrifice by giving something that is difficult to give.

Missionary doctor Helen Roseveare tells a story of an African parent who brought a chicken to her two weeks after she had performed a lifesaving operation on his child. "Some might say that the value of a chicken hardly equaled the value of all the training that had been necessary to enable me to undertake that delicate operation," she says, "and that therefore the gift was inadequate as a thank-offering." Roseveare believes, though, that in God's eyes the two acts were of comparable value. "We had each given all we had," she says. Roseveare says that the most important factor in evaluating the two gifts is the attitude of the heart.

True stewardship is characterized by a willingness to give, even when we don't have much. "When you have no money to contribute, have mercy. . . . We are to give what we have, not what we lack. Charity gives what it can; and when it cannot relieve a burden, it feels sorrow," Jeremy Taylor wrote in *Holy Living*.

The Russian novelist Leo Tolstoy told of a Russian beggar who begged for money during a great famine. Although Tolstoy wished to help the beggar, he had no money. Apologetically, he seized the beggar's hand saying, "Don't be angry with me, brother, I have nothing to give." The beggar disagreed saying, "But you have given me something; you call me brother and that is a greater gift than money."

STEWARDSHIP=SPIRITUAL GROWTH

How does being a good steward enrich your Christian life? What does it do for you spiritually? Stewardship is an extremely important discipline that can greatly advance your relationship with Jesus Christ.

Judy Bates says that stewardship has taught her great spiritual lessons. "Stewardship and trust go hand in hand. As you see the Lord honor His own promises in His Word, you learn to trust Him more and more. You draw closer to Him. You have a greater awareness of the fact that He cares about every aspect of your life, that He is truly watching and with you in the power of Holy Spirit," she says. "He is so faithful. As you follow His teaching, His commands regarding good stewardship, you see more and more of His power, His faithfulness at work in your own life. It's amazing, it's awesome, it's exciting, and it's indescribable."

Perhaps the greatest way we can be good stewards is to be faithful. If we faithfully use our bodies, minds, gifts, time, money, and resources for God's glory, then we not only enrich the lives of others but our lives are blessed far more than we can ever dream. By our faithfulness, we leave an enduring legacy for our children and grandchildren.

And in doing so, we give evidence to the great faith we have in God, a God Who loved us so much that He "gave His only begotten Son" and that we love so much to give the world whatever we can in His name.

PERSONAL QUESTIONS ABOUT STEWARDSHIP

- Do I use my resources for God's glory or selfishly accumulate them for myself?
- Do I give God the leftovers of my time, possessions, and talents or do I give Him my best?
- Do I find it easy to give?

• Do I realize that everything I have is really God's?
• How can I share what I have with others?
• Do I realize that the greatest gift of all may be the time I spend with my spouse, my children, my parents, my friends?
• Can I be a better steward of my time? Do I tithe my time?
• Do I hoard my talents or use them for God's service?
• Have I experienced the joy of tithing?
• Am I being a good steward of my body as well as my mind?

MAKING STEWARDSHIP A PART OF YOUR LIFE

• Thank God that you have money and possessions to give to others.
• Ask God to help you be a steward of your body by eating properly and exercising.
• Ask God to help you be a steward of your mind by taking into it worthwhile messages and also studying to cultivate it.
• Evaluate your stewardship of time this week spent reading your Bible, praying, and worshiping God.
• Evaluate the number of hours you spend each day in worthless pursuits (watching hours of mindless television, etc.).
• Read the parables of Jesus such as the parable of the talents in Matthew 24 to discover what He taught about stewardship.
• Read 2 Corinthians 8 and 9 where Paul encourages Christians to give generously.
• Read Proverbs. The book contains much wisdom on stewardship.
• Ask God to help you schedule your time efficiently so you can devote more time to worthwhile pursuits.
• Pray for God to reveal to you how you can make yourself and your resources available to Him. Then list specific ways that you are going to be obedient in your stewardship.
• If you are in debt, develop a plan to become debt-free.
• Before you make purchases, pray.
• If you do not tithe, start this week. If you do tithe, make an effort to give an offering beyond your tithe.
• Take a genuine interest in another person and give of your time to that person.

• Ask God to reveal to you your spiritual gifts and then become a wise steward of them.
• Use your surplus to help those in need.
• Give an anonymous gift to someone in need.

LIFE APPLICATION VERSE

"But store up for yourselves treasures in heaven, where moth and rust do not destroy, and where thieves do not break in and steal. For where your treasure is, there your heart will be also" (Matt. 6:20).

PRAYER

Give me a generous spirit. I know that You will provide all my needs. Remind me daily that everything I have comes from You. Guide me to tithe my time, possessions, and gifts. Give me discipline to be a wise steward of my body and mind, my entire being. Amen.

11
SERVICE

"Do ordinary things with extraordinary love."—Mother Teresa (1910–1997), missionary to India's poorest of the poor

"Do everything in love" (1 Cor. 16:14).

She felt faint as she pulled the wiggling white maggots loose from a man's limbs. The sick man had been so weakened that flies had laid eggs in his wounds. She had to get every last larvae, scrape the wound, and then disinfect it. When the man's wounds were cleansed and bandaged, Mother Teresa said to her novices, "If I didn't believe with all my heart and soul this man's body is the body of Jesus, I couldn't bear such an abomination for one second."

Mother Teresa taught the world much about being a servant. She epitomized love through her selfless acts of charity.

Born Agnes Gonxha Bojaxhiu to Albanian parents in Yugoslavia, she joined the Sisters of Loreto, an Irish order of missionary nuns. After studying in Ireland, she moved to Calcutta, India, and taught at her order's high school for 17 years.

Sensing God's call to work among the poor, she founded the Missionaries of Charity in 1950. The goals of her fellow nuns and her were to "proclaim the gospel of his love and pity among the poorest of the poor throughout the world." She founded a home for the dying, an orphanage, a leper colony, medical centers, and shelters. Her ministries eventually spread around the world. She received the first Pope John XXIII Peace Prize in 1971, the first Templeton Prize in 1973, and the Nobel Peace Prize in 1979. She accepted all prizes in the name of "the hungry, the naked, the homeless."

The words of Mother Teresa challenge us today to serve: "Remember that it is Christ who works through us—we are merely instruments for service. . . . The fruit of love is service. The fruit of service is peace.

"We serve Jesus in the poor. We nurse Him, feed Him, clothe Him, visit Him, comfort Him in the poor, the abandoned, the sick, the orphans, the dying."

Mother Teresa is one of the most recognizable models of Christian service, but we may find ourselves saying, "I'm not Mother Teresa. I can't go serve in the streets of India." Such thinking is in opposition to our roles as servants in the family of Christ. God calls each of us to serve.

We may not have the capability or opportunity to serve in another country, but there are multitudes of ways that we can serve in Christ's name—through our giving, our vocation, our prayers, our encouragement, and through our acts of service in our families, churches, and communities.

The psalmist said, "O Lord, truly I am your servant" (Psalm 116:16). Jesus said in John 12:26, "Whoever serves me must follow me; and where I am, my servant also will be." The Apostle Paul said in Ephesians 2:10, "We are God's workmanship, created in Christ Jesus to do good works, which God prepared in advance for us to do."

These Scriptural admonitions should challenge us as Christians to say, with a heart of thanksgiving towards God and with an eager and joyful attitude, "As you have given to me, I now want to give to others. I truly am your servant and I will follow you!"

When former President and First Lady Jimmy and Rosalynn Carter left the White House after an election defeat in 1980, they wondered what direction their lives would take. They knew they'd move home to Plains, Georgia, write their memoirs, get their lives back to normal as quickly as possible, and that they would somehow serve.

That form of service soon developed into work with Habitat for Humanity, an organization that builds homes for individuals and families who've never had a decent place to live.

President Carter says that their desire to work with Habitat for Humanity and other service organizations stems from their shared Christian faith. When they help a family build their very own home in South America, inner-city Los Angeles, or Africa, they do so because they are compelled to as Christians. The desire to serve comes directly from Jesus' own example.

"What was the main thrust of Christ's ministry? Did he just sit under a fig tree telling stories, or stand on a mountain explaining theology?" Carter asks. "No. His ministry was tangible proof of his love for everyone, including the sick, the ostracized, and even those who were believed by their neighbors to be suffering the punishment of God for their sins. This was a powerful witness. Christ was a doer, one whose faith took the form of action, not merely words.

"Christ wants us to follow his example by expanding the meaning of forgiveness, service, and love—all in a practical way," he says.

QUALITIES OF A SERVANT

What characteristics should a servant of Christ have?

Charles Swindoll in his book *Improving Your Serve* focused on eight qualities of a servant. He took these from the Beatitudes, the words of Jesus on the Sermon on the Mount, "Blessed are the poor in spirit" (Matt. 5:3–12). Swindoll said these qualities are those of the poor in spirit; mourning, gentle, hungering and thirsting for righteousness, merciful, pure in heart, peacemakers, and persecuted.

In his book *Developing a Servant's Heart*, Charles Stanley singled out six traits taken from Acts 6:2–4, the qualities of those the early church chose to "serve tables": submissiveness, good reputation, full of the Holy Spirit, wisdom, a vision for the work of God, and humility.

A servant possesses all of these traits. Other fundamental qualities paramount to service include:

Love

When Jesus was asked what the greatest commandment was, He essentially answered with a single word, *love.* He said, "Love the Lord your God with all your heart and with all your soul and with all your mind and with all your strength. The second is this: 'Love your neighbor as yourself.' There is no commandment greater than these" (Mark 12:30–31).

We love God and, because we do, we are to love others. What better way to show that love than to serve!

Oswald Chambers said, "To serve God is the deliberate love-gift of a nature that has heard the call of God."

English abolitionist William Wilberforce (1759–1833) believed if we love God, "service becomes our delight; we will seek for more and new opportunities to prove our love."

Nobel Prize–winning missionary Albert Schweitzer (1875–1965) said, "To be glad instruments of God's love in this imperfect world is the service to which man is called."

And the Apostle Paul said in Galatians 5:6, "The only thing that counts is faith expressing itself through love."

When homemaker Kathryn Anderson decided to serve God by going on a missions trip to the west side of Chicago, she never knew what a powerful message in love she would receive. Kathryn and her group led Backyard Bible Clubs in two apartment complexes, one of which was a reputed gang area. On the last day of the trip, a little girl came to the club and attached herself to Kathryn. Kathryn saw in her eyes a hunger for love and, as they readied to leave, the girl jumped into Kathryn's arms and told her she'd miss her.

"This really touched me because I realized that these kids only want to be loved," she said. Kathryn served through the missions trip out of love for the lost in the world and learned, in turn, that that's exactly what the world needs.

Joy

People who serve God are joyful, and their joy reaches over into the lives of others whom they serve. For the Christian, joy is deeper than happiness and does not depend upon external circumstances.

Missionary leader A. B. Simpson (1844–1919) said, "This joy of the Lord is the joy of service. . . . Work for God in the true spirit and in the power of the Holy Spirit is the partnership of His joy. If you wish for a life lifted above a thousand temptations and petty cares, be busy for your Master."

Unselfishness

Service, in its very nature, is selfless. We cannot serve others if we are more concerned about our own well-being or comfort. "In humility consider others better than yourselves. Each of you should look not only to your own interests, but also to the interests of others," Paul wrote in Philippians 2:3–4.

Chuck Swindoll reiterates that verse in *Improving Your Serve* when he says that service is a "sensitive, spontaneous awareness of needs. . . that humility of mind that continually looks for ways to serve and to give."

Oswald Chambers challenged, "Are you willing to spend and be spent; not seeking to be ministered unto, but to minister?"

Obedience

At the heart of service is obedience. If we are truly obedient to the commands of Christ, then we *must* go and serve in His name. There is nothing else we can do!

Jesus commands us to go and serve. He said in John 20:21, "As the Father has sent me, I am sending you."

Many people in the Bible were obedient servants—and not all of them were spiritual "giants" like David and Moses. Paul recognized two little-known, but important, people for their obedient service. Epaphroditus and Onesiphorus both ministered to Paul. He told the Philippian church about Epaphroditus. "Epaphroditus, my brother, fellow worker and fellow soldier, who is also your messenger, whom you sent to take care of my needs. . . .Welcome him in the Lord with great joy, and honor men like him, because he almost died for the work of Christ, risking his life to make up for the help you could not give me" (Phil. 2:25,29).

And Paul wrote to Timothy about Onesiphorus, "May the Lord show mercy to the household of Onesiphorus, because he often refreshed me and was not ashamed of my chains. . . . He searched hard for me until he found me. . . . You know very well in how many ways he helped me in Ephesus" (2 Tim. 1:16–18).

Obedience, says Christian author and pastor Max Lucado, is found in reliable servants. Reliable (*liable* meaning "responsible" and *re* meaning "over and over again") servants are those who are "spurred by a gut-level conviction that they have been called by no one less than God himself."

In his book *God Came Near*, Lucado thanks some of the reliable servants in his life:

"Thank you senior saints for a generation of prayer and forest clearing."

"Thank you teachers for the countless Sunday School lessons, prepared and delivered with tenderness."

"Thank you missionaries for your bravery in sharing the timeless truth in a foreign tongue."

"Thanks to all of you who practice on Monday what you hear on Sunday. You spent selfless hours with orphans, at typewriters, in board meetings, on knees, in hospital wards, away from families, and on assembly lines. It is upon the back of your fidelity that the gospel rides."

MODELS OF SERVICE

Jesus is our foremost model for service. He came to serve. "For even the Son of Man did not come to be served, but to serve, and to give his life a ransom for many" (Mark 10:45).

Jesus preached, taught, healed, fed the hungry, and washed the feet of His disciples. His role of servanthood inspired His followers—(Paul, Andrew, Barnabas, Timothy, Mary, Lydia, and many others) who followed in His stead and served countless lives.

Sometimes we think of Christian service in noble terms, like Mother Teresa working in the Calcutta slums or Elizabeth Fry working tirelessly for prison reform or Amy Carmichael taking in girls who were otherwise destined to be temple prostitutes. We tend to forget that for women like Mother Teresa or Elizabeth Fry or Amy Carmichael, service was often bathing sick lepers; visiting dank, damp prisons; or nursing babies back to health. They lived the words of Jesus, "The greatest among you will be your servant" (Matt. 23:11).

Like Mother Teresa, Elizabeth Fry and Amy Carmichael led lives of spiritual passion, obedience to God, and service to others. Their work took different routes, but each found their place of service and they serve as models for us today.

Elizabeth Fry

The tall serene woman wearing the plain Quaker dress was appalled after encountering the foul odors and obscene language of the prison. She discovered 300 women, some almost naked, with their children crowded into four dank rooms, without beds or bedding or extra clothing, guarded by one male attendant and his son. She witnessed women begging for money so they could buy liquor. She looked into the hopeless faces of many women who had been thrown into prison because they had fallen in debt after their husbands had died or had left them.

This was what Elizabeth Fry (1780–1845) observed in 1813 on her first trip to the notorious Newgate Prison near her London home.

The mother of 11 children, she was awakened by her Christian faith to inject greater humanity into a largely inhumane system. She used efforts similar to those Charles Colson successfully uses in his prison ministry today. She instilled in the women the belief that holiness and strength come from faith. In 1817 she organized a group of Quaker women to regularly visit the prisoners. In the book *Dates with Destiny*, 1817 is cited as one of the most important dates in church history because it marked a pivotal year in the history of crime and punishment. The efforts of Elizabeth and her group transformed life behind bars for women. The prisoners discovered a newfound faith through Bible studies and a useful skill in sewing classes.

Giving testimony in the British House of Commons, she awakened the need for reform, leading to the Prison Act of 1823. She gained international fame by inspecting jails in France, Switzerland, Germany, Belgium, Holland, Denmark, and Russia.

As she lay dying, Elizabeth said, "I can say one thing—since my heart was touched at seventeen years old I believe I never have awakened from sleep, in sickness or in health, by day or by night, without my first waking thought being how best I might serve my Lord."

What a legacy to inspire us today!

Amy Carmichael

Prenna was a child of 7 who was forced to live in a Hindu temple. Once she had run away 20 miles, but was brought back, and her hands branded with hot irons. She determined to run away again and found her way into the sanctuary of the Presbyterian missionary's bungalow.

Amy Carmichael (1867–1951) and her companions kept Prenna in 1901. Soon other temple runaways and abandoned children joined her. Amy focused her efforts on children such as Prenna who were to be dedicated as Hindu temple prostitutes. She founded the Dohnavur Fellowship with more than 800 children in three homes, a hospital, and evangelistic work.

A prolific author, she wrote 35 books, including *Things As They Are* (1903), which shocked many readers with its harsh truths about ministering in a foreign culture. Badly injured in a fall in 1931, she became an invalid but continued to write.

"Ask not how little but how much can love give" became the principle that governed her life. "Oh, to care, and oh for power to make others care," she once wrote, "not less, but far, far more!" The Irish missionary served with the Church of England Zenana Missionary Society for 56 years, without a furlough.

Christians today continue in the steps of Elizabeth Fry and Amy Carmichael as they serve Christ in innumerable ways. They feed the hungry at community soup kitchens; they pray for friends and family members and unknown strangers; they teach Sunday School; they encourage and counsel others; they do what they can in any way they can.

Immediately following the September 11, 2001, terrorist attacks on New York City and Washington, D. C., thousands of volunteers poured into the areas of destruction offering many different forms of service. Among them were Christians from many different churches and ministry groups. They counseled victims, gave water and food to rescue workers, prayed with the hurt and grieving, provided donations of goods, witnessed to victims about God's love and grace, and offered medical services.

At a time when the nation was grieving, Christians served their fellow Americans out of love and duty. It is what Christians are called to do all the time!

USING OUR GIFTS FOR SERVICE

God told Jeremiah that He had set him apart for His service. "'Before I formed you in the womb I knew you, before you were born I set you apart; I appointed you as a prophet to the nations'" (Jer. 1:5). Like Jeremiah, God sets us apart for His service.

The New Testament teaches, "Each one should use whatever gift he has received to serve others, faithfully administering God's grace in its various forms. . . . If anyone serves, he should do it with the strength God provides, so that in all things God may be praised through Jesus Christ" (1 Peter 4:10–11).

God gives all Christians spiritual gifts to serve Him and others.

English pastor Charles Spurgeon said, "All the strength supplied to us by our gracious God is meant for service."

Our lives in service to God can take many forms. "Whatever you do, work at it with all your heart, as working for the Lord, not for men, since you know that you will receive an inheritance from the Lord as a reward. It is the Lord Christ you are serving" (Col. 3:23).

John Stott, in his book *Christian Basics,* says Christian service involves the home, job, church, community, and the world. We are to find our place in these areas by being servants. How can we find our place, though, if we don't know what our gifts are? How do we discover the spiritual gifts that God has given us?

Author Barbara Joiner is passionate about spiritual gifts. She's written books and speaks to women's conferences and missions groups about the topic. She especially loves to help women determine what their gifts are.

Barbara believes that confusion often comes in comparing talents and spiritual gifts; they are quite different, she says. "Talents are not spiritual gifts. Talents are given to every person, both Christians and non-Christians," Barbara says. "Both talents and spiritual gifts come from the Lord. But talents are natural gifts. Spiritual gifts are supernatural. Christians are to use their spiritual gifts in service for others."

Once you know what spiritual gift (or gifts) you possess, the important thing is to put it (or them) to use for others. Barbara lists the spiritual gifts as prophecy, service, teaching, exhorting, sharing, leading, mercy, love, enthusiasm, hope, prayer, and hospitality.

"Use is the key," Barbara says. "Ask yourself, How can I use my gifts? Then find ways you can use your gifts. Do you have the gift of hospitality? Then throw a party for some handicapped children in your community. Do you have the gift of teaching? Use that gift to teach an international to read."

Realize that at the moment you became a believer, God gave you gifts; find out what your gifts are; then put those gifts to use!

Our service takes different forms, some of which follow.

Praying

What greater power is there on earth and in heaven than the power of prayer? Unfortunately, prayer may sometimes seem less important than gifts that are more outwardly visible. Realize, though, that no other actions are possible without the power of prayer behind them.

Missionary Mary Slessor said, "Prayer is the greatest power God has put into our hands for service—praying is harder work than doing, at least I find it so."

S. D. Gordon said in his book *Quiet Talks on Prayer*, "Intercession is service: the chief service of a life on God's plan."

John Hyde (1865–1912) found his gift and used it. He was one of the greatest pray-ers in Christian history. Known as Praying Hyde, he would sometimes pray for over 40 hours on his knees. He went to the Punjab region of India as a Presbyterian missionary in 1892. Soon after he arrived in India, he started praying for revival. He learned several of the local languages and taught Bible in a boys' high school. He often traveled to remote villages leading people to Christ and praying with converts.

In July 1904 he began a 30-day prayer vigil for a spiritual life convention to be held in August in Sialkot, India. Vigilant, intensive praying by the participants led to many conversions as revival broke out. For years John led prayer sessions for the annual conventions. Completely worn out by his labor, he returned to New York in 1911 and died the next year. His last words were "Bol Yisu Masih, Ki Jai!" (Shout the victory of Jesus Christ!).

Like John Hyde, we can further God's kingdom when we pray. Pray for others through intercessory prayer; speak to God on the behalf of friends, family members, acquaintances, even strangers. And pray for the service of others, as they use their gifts in more visible ways such as giving and doing.

Giving

Giving of our time, money, and possessions is a wonderful service. Giving can take many forms. It may mean comforting a bereaved widow, helping a family with a special-needs child, placing money in the offering plate, or giving a cup of water to someone who is thirsty.

Once King David was thirsty and wanted a drink from a well. Three of his high-ranking soldiers went behind enemy lines to get him a drink of water. David was so moved that they risked their lives for him that he couldn't drink the water. He offered it to God instead (1 Chron. 11:17–19).

Who can forget the Bible story of the widow's mite? Although she gave so little in comparison to the amounts others gave, she actually gave more than the others because she gave all she had. Any giving we are able to do, whether it's much or little, is a true service to God.

Going/Doing

"Do all the good you can, by all the means you can, in all the ways you can, in all the places you can, at all the times you can, to all the people you can, as long as ever you can," advised John Wesley. Service, then, can also come in the very visible form of going and doing.

Oswald Chambers once said, "The real test of the saint is not preaching the gospel, but washing disciples' feet, that is, doing the things that do not count in the actual estimate of men but count everything in the estimate of God."

How can you serve God by going and doing? How can you "wash feet" in your neighborhood and community today?

Encouraging

Paul said in Hebrews 10:24, "And let us consider how we may spur one another on toward love and good deeds."

The New Testament character Barnabas was a great encourager. In fact, his name meant "son of encouragement" (Acts 4:36). He once "sold a field he owned and brought the money and put it at the apostles' feet" (Acts 4:37). We find Barnabas in another encouraging role when he took Paul to the apostles in Jerusalem and spoke up on Paul's behalf (Acts 9:27). (Some people were unsure of Paul's sincerity because before his conversion he had persecuted Christians.) Barnabas also encouraged Paul and Mark even when they made mistakes and gave them another chance. Barnabas next sent relief offerings to Judea (Acts 11:29–30). It seems that each time the New Testament mentions Barnabas, he was truly living up to his name!

How can we be sons and daughters of encouragement, like Barnabas? Write letters or phone a friend in need; thank a church member who does an often thankless volunteer job; give a hug or pat on the back to someone who needs it; let someone in grief know that you are praying for them; give money to a needy family.

Showing Hospitality

Some Christians serve through the gift of hospitality. They immediately make someone feel welcome in an unfamiliar place; they love to invite others into their homes for meals and Bible study; they open their homes to visiting missionaries; they leave the door open for youth in their church.

Emilie Barnes, the author of such books as *The Heart of Loveliness* and *15 Minutes Alone with God*, reminds us that anyone can share hospitality. She tells of her mother, who at 77 lived in a one-room efficiency apartment in a high-rise retirement complex. And although she had limited resources, she greeted visitors with gladness and enthusiasm.

"She continually shared hospitality with a cup of tea, a cookie, a piece of carrot cake, or some banana bread," Emilie says. "Her guests always felt special sipping tea in a real china teacup, eating cookies placed on a pretty plate with a paper doily, and enjoying a few flowers on the table with a lit candle."

Emilie says that many people today "grumble" at the thought of having people to their homes, but she encourages them to do so. She reminds us that even Jesus fed people before He preached to them. "Having friends in our home gives us the opportunity to let them see

Jesus in us, to feel our spirits, to be touched by our love and caring," she says. "Many doors have been opened in the hearts of our friends when we've shared a meal together."

OUR WORK AS SERVICE

An area of service we often neglect is the service we can do in our workplace. Are you a teacher? A painter? An accountant? A nurse? A doctor? A stay-at-home mother? An auto worker? A business owner? You can use your vocation to reach out in service to others.

George Washington Carver (1861?–1943) was a scientist. But what a scientist! Biddy Chambers was a stenographer. But what a stenographer!

A Scientist at Work for God

He said that God led him to discover 300 products from the peanut including lard, cheese, flour, soap, and plastics. From the sweet potato he made 100 discoveries, among them starch, vinegar, molasses, and ink.

George Washington Carver was one of the most remarkable Americans who ever lived. Born as a slave in Diamond Grove, Missouri, he was separated from his mother when she was abducted from Moses Carver, her master, by the Ku Klux Klan and sold to new owners. Raised by Moses Carver, George became a Christian at the age of 10. "God just came into my heart one afternoon while I was alone in the loft of our big barn," George recalled later in life. "That was my simple conversion, and I have tried to keep the faith."

Keep the faith he did. After graduating with a master of agriculture degree from Iowa State College, he joined the faculty of Tuskegee Institute in Tuskegee, Alabama, after an invitation from founder Booker T. Washington. George served 47 years, shaping the lives of countless students and dramatically influencing farming in the South and the economy of America while at the same time fighting racial prejudice.

He once wrote of his students, "I want them to find Jesus. . . . How I long for each one to walk and talk with the Great Creator through the things he has created." In 1939 he received the Roosevelt Medal for Outstanding Contribution to Southern Agriculture. At his death he was buried with the epitaph, "He could have added fortune to fame, but caring for neither, he found happiness and honor in being helpful to the world."

A Stenographer at Work for God

She sat quietly in his congregations and took notes on her husband's messages. She could write quickly using shorthand she had learned being a stenographer.

We know very little about her except she was a wife, mother, and a stenographer. She may have had some personal ambitions, but we don't know what they were. What we do know is that she used her skill to make her husband, Oswald Chambers, the most loved devotional writer in the world.

Baptist evangelist Oswald Chambers was converted after hearing Charles Spurgeon preach. After training for the ministry in western Scotland, he became widely known as a preacher. In 1911 he became principal of the Bible Training College, Clapham Common, London. In 1915 during World War I he worked with the British troops in Egypt in connection with the YMCA. He was a beloved chaplain who effectively conveyed the gospel with the soldiers. Throughout his ministry, Biddy sat quietly in the background taking notes on his messages. In 1917 Oswald died at the age of 43 following complications from an appendectomy. Biddy, widowed at the age of 34 with a young daughter, sent a telegram to her family and friends that read simply, "OSWALD IN HIS PRESENCE."

After returning home to England, she put together the notes she had recorded from her husband's many sermons into books, 50 books in all! *My Utmost for His Highes*t is the most widely read. All the books bear her husband's name but only her initials.

George Washington Carver and Biddy Chambers represent all the people around us today who use their abilities to serve others.

THE IMPORTANCE OF SERVICE

As we reach out in service, whether it's through our jobs, our prayers, our volunteer work, or our giving, no task is too menial or too small. All service in the name of Christ is meaningful. When we serve, no matter what the task, we are following in the steps of Jesus. English poet Robert Browning (1812–1889) wisely said, "All service ranks the same with God."

Author Anita Corrine Donihue said, "Thank You for calling me. No matter the cost, help me always to be a servant You can be pleased with."

Despite this high calling from God, most people today don't want to be servants. They want to be served. Ours is a self-serving society. "We Christians like to refer to ourselves as servants, but we are seldom content to be treated as servants," wrote Henry Blackaby in *Experiencing God Day by Day*. "The world will estimate your importance by the number of people serving you; God is more concerned with the number of people you are serving."

We remember the Mother Teresas, the Amy Carmichaels, and the George Washington Carvers of the world because they devoted their lives to service. We also remember our parents, neighbors, missionaries, and countless others because they used their gifts for God's glory. We follow in their footsteps as we reach out in love to serve a neighborhood, a community, a nation, and a world that needs to know of God's great grace.

"A life of service leaves a legacy of influence, the greater the service, the greater the legacy," wrote Charles Stanley in *Developing a Servant's Heart*.

May we change the world by the legacies of service we leave.

PERSONAL QUESTIONS ABOUT SERVICE

- How do I serve others daily?
- What spiritual gifts has God given me?
- Do I use my gifts in serving others?
- Which of these acts of service do I practice on a regular basis: praying, giving, going/doing, encouraging, hospitality?

• Do I serve God through my work?
• Do I find joy in serving?
• Do others see Jesus through my actions and lifestyle?
• Would it help me to take the focus off of my own problems by helping others?

MAKING SERVICE A PART OF YOUR LIFE

• Spend time with God daily asking Him how you can serve Him. Then say yes to His guidance.
• Read Psalms 116 and 118 and meditate on what David says about being a servant.
• Volunteer at a soup kitchen or a ministry center. Be attentive and sensitive to the needs of people you meet.
• Don't get so busy serving others that you forget to serve your family.
• Spend a whole day being a "servant" to your family in actions and attitude.
• If you are going through a difficult time, reach out to a sick, lonely, or bereaved friend or stranger.
• Pray for opportunities to serve through your church's ministries.
• Tell your pastor that your house is available for guest speakers to stay in.
• Pray daily that God will place you in the right place to serve others.
• Always look for ways you can serve.
• Be a good listener.
• Build relationships with family members, co-workers, people of other races and cultures.
• Do one anonymous good deed a week.
• Reach out to a stranger.
• Call someone who is lonely. Ask the person out for lunch, or take him or her some flowers.
• Do something special for someone who usually serves you.
• Use your vacation this year volunteering for a missions trip, building homes for the underprivileged, or working in a soup kitchen.

LIFE APPLICATION VERSE

"Each one should use whatever gift he has received to serve others, faithfully administering God's grace in its various forms" (1 Peter 4:10).

PRAYER

Thank You, God, for the opportunity and privilege that I have to serve others. Empower me daily to use my gifts to meet needs in my family, community, and the world. May my words and actions always reflect Jesus and His love. Amen.

12
SACRIFICE

"I would I had a thousand lives that I might give them to the women of China."
—Lottie Moon (1840–1912), American missionary to China

"I appeal to you therefore, brothers and sisters, by the mercies of God, to present your bodies as a living sacrifice, holy and acceptable to God, which is your spiritual worship" (Rom. 12:1 NRSV).

A severe famine hit the Shantung Province. Many people were starving. She fed hundreds at her doorstep, but she refused to eat. Physically exhausted, she started the long journey home to America.

It was Christmas Eve 1912. Because she gave away all her money and food, Southern Baptist missionary Lottie Moon (1840–1912) died of starvation aboard ship in the harbor of Kobe, Japan.

Lottie Moon's life, as well as her death, was characterized by sacrifice.

Lottie was born on December 12, 1840, near Scottsville, Virginia. One of the first southern women to receive a master's degree, she was considered "the best educated and most cultured woman in the South" when she sailed to China in 1873. Instead of living a comfortable life in America, she dedicated her life to sacrificial service among the women of North China.

She spent most of her 40 years in women's work at Tengchow. There in her living room she organized the North China Woman's Missionary Union. For 9 years she lived at Pingtu evangelizing where no woman missionary had ever gone. She served as a counselor, comforter, teacher, and minister to the people she loved.

Lottie had a great love for the Chinese, and they for her. A fellow missionary said of her, "We all love her. And how the Chinese love her is beautiful to see."

Lottie's words reflect her attitude about sacrifice: "I have lived right down among the people, and I know they can be won by loving self-sacrifice on the part of the missionaries."

"Let them [missionaries] come rejoicing to sacrifice for that Lord and Master who so freely gave himself for them."

Another missionary wrote of Lottie's sacrifice: "She makes very little ado about her sacrifices. I think I might safely say that no missionary is making greater sacrifices than she is making."

Initiated by Lottie in December 1887 (and named for her after her death), the Lottie Moon Christmas Offering for International Missions is a fitting legacy of her sacrifice.

After Lottie's death from starvation, the Chinese Christians at Tengchow spent 3 years gathering the love gifts that went into a marble stone monument for her. The three lines on it read: "1915; A Monument to bequeath the love of Miss Lottie Moon, an American missionary; The Tengchow church remembers forever."

Lottie Moon presented her body "as a living sacrifice." Her legacy of sacrifice literally changed the world through the offering bearing her name, which goes entirely for work in international missions. It has raised over a billion dollars, and millions of lives have been changed through the ministries it supports.

We may read of Lottie Moon's life and wonder how we could ever live lives of sacrifice when compared to hers. "I live quite comfortably," you may say. "I don't sacrifice like Lottie Moon did or like missionaries do in remote parts of the world."

Sacrifice, though, can take many forms. It can mean dying in service for Christ, as it did for Lottie Moon. It can mean facing persecution as a Christian, as it does for many men, women, and children around the world today. But it can also have other meanings.

The 11 practices explored in the preceding chapters, in fact, are all ways Christians can live a life consecrated to God. When practiced obediently and conscientiously, they can result in a sacrificial offering that is pleasing to God.

We can pray unceasingly for others.

We can devote quality and quantity time to Bible study, giving other pursuits to study God's Word.

We can invest the time it takes to worship God privately and corporately.

We can witness boldly to both friends and strangers.

We can commit time to solitude to be alone with God.

We can journal our thoughts and feelings, our prayers and gleanings from the Bible—all of which require a sacrifice of time.

We can give up other pursuits to immerse ourselves in good Christian literature and Bible studies.

We can spend time seeking guidance from God.

We can strive for simplicity, putting God first in our lives and eliminating other things that keep us from totally giving ourselves to Him.

We can give generously of our time, gifts, resources, body, and mind to be good stewards.

Finally, we can serve others, which may result in physical and mental exhaustion, and even injury or loss of life.

WHAT DOES SACRIFICE MEAN?

A dictionary definition of sacrifice is "a loss sustained in the accomplishment of or as the result of something."

Mother Teresa insightfully said, "You must give what will cost you something."

It might mean giving your life; it could mean being "spent" for the Lord through your service to others. It might mean giving up your time to accomplish God's work. It might mean losing friendships because of your commitment to God. It might mean giving up favorite pastimes for godly pursuits. Whenever you sacrifice, it will cost you something, but the heavenly reward and peace of mind surpass anything the world can give.

Retired businesswoman Jo Edmonson learned about sacrifice after losing two of the most important things in her life, her husband and, soon after, her business. Through these losses Jo allowed God to teach her important truths and draw closer to Him.

After a long illness, Jo's husband, Gaston, died of lung cancer. She says she remembers feeling lost and alone after his death; she didn't know how she would go on in a practical way. She fell back on the arts and crafts shop she owned as a way to deal with the loss.

Then, 5 years later, the store was destroyed by fire. "I now know that the shop burning down was a blessing, although I didn't know it at the time," Jo says. "I felt like I was sacrificing so much, that I was giving up so much. But I now know that it was part of God's plan."

The shop consumed so much of her time, energy, and finances that her thoughts were not on what really mattered. Today, she feels blessed that she can spend her energy on more important matters. She serves others through her church's program that provides food and clothing for the less fortunate; and she uses her arts ability to help others in a personal way, instead of as a means to make money.

So, what she saw as a sacrifice was actually not one at all. "People would look at me and feel sorry for me, thinking of how much I had lost," she says. "But it wasn't a loss at all."

WHAT DOES THE BIBLE SAY ABOUT SACRIFICE?

The Bible addresses sacrifice in both the physical and the spiritual senses.

Jesus spoke of the ultimate human sacrifice when He said, "Greater love has no one than this, that he lay down his life for his friends" (John 15:13); and again when He said, "If you give up your life for me and for the good news, you will save it. . . . Don't be ashamed of me and my message among these . . . sinful people" (Mark 8:35,38 CEV).

Paul spoke often of suffering and sacrificing for Christ, such as when he wrote to Timothy: "Because I preach the Good News, I am suffering. . . . I am willing to endure anything if it will bring salvation and eternal glory in Christ Jesus to those God has chosen" (2 Tim. 2:9–10 NLT).

The Bible also talks of the sacrifice of our hearts and minds and souls; we are to give everything over to God. Only then will He be pleased with what we have to offer Him. "The sacrifice acceptable to God is a broken spirit; a broken and contrite heart" (Psalm 51:17).

The writer of Hebrews repeated this message. "And do not forget to do good and to share with others, for with such sacrifices God is pleased" (Heb. 13:16).

Many biblical figures modeled sacrificial living and dying. Many of the original apostles and later disciples died for their faith; even one who lived, John, was tortured and sent into exile. Their stories still inspire us today to lead lives of sacrifice. Paul was beheaded in Rome in A.D. 65; Stephen was stoned to death; Andrew was crucified; Matthew was beheaded; Jude was beaten to death; Thomas was killed by spears in India; many others were killed in violent ways while staying adamant and strong in their faith.

And Jesus, of course, paid the ultimate sacrifice when He voluntarily died for our sins. He sacrificed His rights as God, became a man, lived sacrificially on earth for 33 years, and then died that we all might live. When living our lives in light of this amazing sacrifice, we are challenged to ask ourselves: What can I give up for this Jesus Who loved me so much?

SACRIFICING THEIR LIVES

She performed all surgeries in her bathroom. Once after amputating the leg of a Chinese man, she determined he needed skin grafts. When asked about the scars on her own leg, she brushed away the question. A nurse later complained that a skin graft for the "good-for-nothing coolie" had come from the doctor's own leg.

Eleanor Chestnut (?–1905), a Presbyterian medical missionary to China, epitomized agape love and sacrificial living, qualities she learned early in life. She wore missionary castoffs to get through Park College in Missouri. While at Chicago's Woman's Medical College, she lived in an attic and ate mostly oatmeal.

While building a women's hospital in Lien-chou, she lived on $1.50 a month so the remainder of her salary could go for bricks. When her missionary board insisted on repaying her, she refused saying, "It will spoil all my fun."

On October 28, 1905, she and other missionaries were working at the hospital when a mob attacked. After alerting authorities, she could have escaped, but she returned to aid others. Her last heroic act was to tear strips from her dress to use as a bandage for a wounded boy in the crowd.

Eleanor's story calls to mind the story of the good Samaritan: "But a Samaritan, as he traveled, came where the man was; and when he saw him, he took pity on him. He went to him and bandaged his wounds, pouring on oil and wine" (Luke 10:33–34). In her compassion, she gave the supreme sacrifice.

Eric Liddell is another historical figure who lived and died in a sacrificial manner.

A note slipped into his hand before he ran the 400-meter race at the 1924 Paris Olympics reminded him of the passage in 1 Samuel. "Those who honor me I will honor" (1 Sam. 2:30).

Before this race, Eric Liddell (1902–1945) had truly honored God. He had refused to compete in the 100-meter race that he had trained for because the event was held on a Sunday. Criticized by many for being legalistic, Eric stuck to his convictions. He entered the 200-meter race winning a bronze medal and the 400-meter for which he won a gold, broke the world record, and received worldwide honors.

The 1981 Oscar-winning movie *Chariots of Fire*, which chronicled his victory, brought renewed fame to "Scotland's most famous athlete." The movie, though, told only part of his story.

Graduating from Edinburgh University in 1925, Eric followed in his missionary father's steps and joined the London Missionary Society as a teacher at the Tientsin Anglo-Chinese Christian College. He served there and as a rural evangelist near Siachang until the Japanese interned him in a camp in 1943. In prison he served others energetically. Totally expending himself and not realizing he had a brain tumor, he died in February 1945.

Eric Liddell took every opportunity to honor Christ as an athlete, missionary, and prisoner. Among the last words of one of the twentieth century's most active Christians were these: "It's complete surrender." How appropriate for one who had completely surrendered his life to God's will!

Another person who sacrificed his life was Dietrich Bonhoeffer (1906–1945), the great German Lutheran theologian who refused obedience to Hitler in World War II. Arrested by the gestapo in 1943 because of his involvement in the plot against Hitler, he won the respect of guards and fellow prisoners for his fearless Christian testimony. Hanged at the Flossenburg concentration camp, he died less than a month before the collapse of the deadly regime. A camp doctor who had to confirm his death said of him, "In the almost fifty years that I worked as a doctor, I have hardly ever seen a man die so entirely submissive to the will of God."

Dietrich Bonhoeffer's influence will never die. His classic book *The Cost of Discipleship* will reverberate through the generations as he challenges us not to embrace "cheap grace" but "costly grace." He said, "Cheap grace is grace without discipleship. . . . Costly grace is the gospel which must be sought again and again, the gift which must be asked for, the door at which a man must knock." He continues, "It is costly because it costs a man his life, and it is grace because it gives a man the only true life."

In the centuries since Jesus' death, the world has seen thousands of Christians die for their faith. And this ultimate sacrifice continues today. According to the *World Christian Encyclopedia,* almost 156,000 Christians around the world were martyred in 1998, and the persecution continues today.

Tom White, an American Christian who covertly distributed more than 400,000 pieces of gospel literature to Cuba in the 1970s, crash-landed his plane during a night drop and was arrested. He was interrogated about his work and thrown into solitary confinement.

During his nights in the cold, completely dark cell, Tom found solace in singing. "As the levels of punishment grew more severe, so did the intensity of spiritual warfare," Tom remembers. "I started singing that great hymn, 'A Mighty Fortress Is Our God.' I sang 'Jesus Loves Me,' Bible choruses, every Christian song I could remember. I was no longer conscious of the cold, only of Jesus. With eyes closed, my head barely touching the wall, I whistled, sang, even imitated a trumpet blasting out praises to the Lord."

Tom was eventually released to a regular prison, where he was able to worship with fellow Christians. Then an international campaign for his release freed him from captivity.

Today, Tom educates the world about persecution and sacrifice as the US director for the Voice of the Martyrs. In his many travels with the organization, Tom has seen Christians who have suffered much more than he did. One man in Vietnam had a lasting influence on him. The man told him, "Suffering is not the worst thing that can happen to us. Disobedience to God is the worst thing."

LIVING SACRIFICIAL LIVES

We may not be called to give up our lives for Christ, but we can live our lives in sacrificial ways. One of the best ways to do this is to serve others sacrificially.

"So faith, hope, love abide, these three; but the greatest of these is love" (1 Cor. 13:13 RSV). Our love for others should be so great that we sacrifice for them.

Many people throughout history have embodied sacrificial living. One was poor, female, illiterate, black, and a slave. But she overcame these great barriers to become the symbol of a woman willing to sacrifice her life for a cause greater than herself. She lived the verse, "Not by might nor by power, but by my Spirit, says the Lord Almighty" (Zech. 4:6).

Harriet Tubman (1821?–1913), known as the Moses of her people, escaped from slavery and headed to the North in 1849. She joined the abolitionist cause and became a conductor on the Underground Railroad—the secret organization that helped southern slaves escape to freedom. Over 10 years she made at least 15 expeditions into Maryland personally escorting hundreds of runaway slaves. Despite being in danger of her life (there were large rewards for her capture) she worked tirelessly. During the Civil War she served as a scout, spy, and nurse with the Union army. After the war she set up schools for blacks and established a home for the elderly in Auburn, New York.

Harriet's deep Christian faith enabled her to do her courageous work. She trusted God completely and knew that apart from God working within her she could do nothing. She told her biographer, Sarah Bradford, that she talked with God, and He talked with her every day of her life. She said, "I prayed all the time, about my work, everywhere; I was always talking to the Lord." She trusted God to take care of her as she went on her journeys to personally rescue slaves.

Not surprisingly, one of her favorite Bible verses was Isaiah 16:3, "Hide the fugitives, do not betray the refugees." God helped her with finances, with clothes, and sometimes with strong premonitions about impending danger. She said, "Just so long as he wanted to use me, he would take care of me. . . . I always told him, 'I'm going to hold steady on to you, and you've got to see me through.'" He always did get her through. She died at the age of 93 singing "Swing Low, Sweet Chariot."

After examining the lives of people such as Harriet Tubman or Tom White, we may be compelled to ask how we can serve others in a sacrificial way.

Can you give up your time to serve in a special church or community ministry? Can you sacrifice your money, or some specific luxury, to help others? Can you sacrifice your vacation to go on a missions trip instead?

Sacrificial living is something God expects us to do!

ATTITUDE TOWARD SACRIFICE

Though Christians throughout the ages have made sacrifices, many would not consider their manner of living or lifestyle a sacrifice.

Hudson Taylor, founder of the China Inland Mission, said, "I never made a sacrifice." His biographer son said Hudson's was a life in which sacrifice was "certainly not lacking"; but "he came to see that giving up is inevitably receiving, when one is dealing heart to heart with God." Hudson humbly said of his decades of work, "Unspeakable joy all day long and every day, was my happy experience. . . . All I had to do was joyful service."

Christians today often have the same attitude.

Carrie and Lance Borden serve as Southern Baptist missionaries to Austria; they say that the hardest part of their service is leaving their families behind in the United States. They realize this is a sacrifice. Their children, after all, are unable to see their grandparents except on rare stateside assignments, but it does not make them stop wanting to serve.

"Our families are called to release us into God's care in foreign places," Carrie says. "It is heartwrenching each time we part, but it is worth it to part for His sake."

Carrie and her family rely on Exodus 14:15 for comfort whenever they feel as if they're sacrificing too much. "If they had been thinking of the country they had left, they would have had opportunity to return. Instead, they were longing for a better country—a heavenly one."

The September 11, 2001, attack on the World Trade Center reiterated this unwavering call to service when numerous firemen, policemen, and emergency workers rushed into harm's way in hopes of saving others. When asked whether they'd risk their own lives again, rescue workers repeatedly answered, "It's our job. We have to do this."

Friends and colleagues of Father Mychal Judge say he was doing what he loved doing best when he died at the World Trade Center. Judge, a Franciscan priest and fire department chaplain, died while administering last rites to a victim; falling debris struck and killed him. His sacrifice was exemplary of his life, people said. "He was a priest for all people. He worked with the poor and the police and AIDS patients and the firemen," said Father Brian Jordan.

Do our lives display a similar attitude? Do we see sacrifice as a necessary ingredient for our spiritual growth?

Missionary leader A. B. Simpson said: "Without the spirit of self-sacrifice, no work can be glorious. . . . We must be willing to endure hardness as good soldiers of Jesus Christ. We must be indifferent to popularity and human praise. . . . We must be glad to be the companions of the lowly and despised, to face toil, hardship or even death and to count all things but loss for Christ and His kingdom."

And do our lives reflect a joyful attitude about sacrifice? As Christians, we know that sacrifice, even difficult and painful times of suffering, can help us grow.

Kay Arthur, an author and Bible study leader, believes that we can learn to experience joy in the midst of our sacrifice. She explains it like this: "Hebrews 13 says that Jesus suffered outside the gate. In other words, He was put with the criminals outside the gate. It says that we are to go out there with Him—outside the city where He is, so to speak.

"Remember that this life is just temporal, we are looking at the eternal—the city that is to come! So we're to offer to God, continually, a sacrifice of praise."

Kay says that a sacrifice is something you put on the altar and to death. "So, you don't feel like praising God, but you sacrifice your feeling and you act in faith. When you do that, then God meets you at that point of obedience," she says. "You have done what is right. You have trusted God and that pleases God. That will change the way you feel!"

Rejoice, then, in the sacrifices you can make for God! You don't need that extra $100? You can give it to missions? That's great news!

You don't need to sell your van? You want to donate it instead to the church? Have joy in that decision! You want to give your two weeks of vacation to missions work in the inner city? What a wonderful experience you will have! You want to sacrifice a bad habit so you can draw closer to God? Hallelujah!

Scottish author George MacDonald said, "A multitude of successive small sacrifices may work more good in the world than many a larger one." Perhaps he was referring to doing things day in and day out that are sacrificial in nature.

How can we do that today? In light of the great sacrifices made over the centuries, how can we offer a sacrifice that is pleasing to God? How can we begin practicing "small" sacrifices in our lives?

PERSONAL QUESTIONS ABOUT SACRIFICE

• Have I ever considered Paul's admonition in Romans 12:1 to offer my body as a "living sacrifice"?
• What is my attitude about sacrifice?
• Where can I sacrificially serve God?
• Would I be willing to lay down my life for a friend?
• Am I sacrificially giving of myself to help others?
• Am I sacrificing my time?
• Am I sacrificing my possessions?
• Am I using my gifts and talents sacrificially?

MAKING SACRIFICE PART OF YOUR LIFE

• Ask God to show you how you can practice Romans 12:1 each day.
• Pray that God will show you daily how to live a life of stewardship that reflects sacrifice on your part.
• Thank God for all the sacrifices Christians have made and continue to make each day.
• Thank God for the examples of Christian martyrs throughout history.
• Read biographies of missionaries and other men and women of God who have given sacrificially of themselves.
• Pray daily for those whose lives are in jeopardy each day because of their faith.

- Give away something that you treasure.
- Do a good deed for someone secretly.

LIFE APPLICATION VERSE

"I appeal to you therefore, brothers and sisters, by the mercies of God, to present your bodies as a living sacrifice, holy and acceptable to God, which is your spiritual worship" (Rom. 12:1 NRSV).

PRAYER

Worthy Lord, today and every day, help me to honor You with my life, everything that I do and say. May I daily exhibit agape love to those around me. Help me cultivate and use all disciplines of my spiritual life (prayer, Bible study, worship, witnessing, solitude, journaling, personal study, guidance, simplicity, stewardship, and service) as a sacrifice to You. Amen.

Recommended Resources

Spiritual Disciplines

Foster, Richard J. *Celebration of Discipline, The.* 3d. ed. San Francisco: HarperSan-Francisco, 1988.

Foster, Richard J., and Emilie Griffin, eds. *Spiritual Classics.* San Francisco: Harper-SanFrancisco, 2000.

Harkness, Allan. *Seeds of Spiritual Growth.* Downers Grove, IL: InterVarsity Press, 2001.

Newenhuyse, Elizabeth Cody. *God, I Know You're Here Somewhere.* Minneapolis: Bethany House Publishers, 1996.

Ortlund, Anne. *The Disciplines of the Beautiful Woman.* Nashville: Word Publishing Group, 1984.

______. *Disciplines of the Heart.* Nashville: Word Publishing Group, 1987.

Watkins, William D. *The Busy Christian's Guide to Experiencing God More.* Ann Arbor, MI: Servant Publications, 1997. Out of print.

Whitney, Donald. *Spiritual Disciplines for the Christian Life.* Colorado Springs: Nav-Press Publishing Group, 1991.

Willard, Dallas. *The Spirit of the Disciplines.* Reprint, San Francisco: HarperSanFrancisco, 1991.

Prayer

Arthur, Kay. *Lord, Teach Me to Pray in 28 Days.* Eugene, OR: Harvest House Publishers, 2001.

Bounds, E. M. *The Complete Words of E. M. Bounds on Prayer.* Grand Rapids, MI: Baker Book House, 1990.

Christenson, Evelyn. *What Happens When Women Pray.* Colorado Springs: Chariot/Victor Publishing, 1992.

Copeland, Germaine. *Prayers That Avail Much.* Tulsa, OK: Harrison House, Inc., 1999.

Donihue, Anita C. *When I'm on My Knees.* Uhrichsville, OH: Barbour Publishing, Inc., 1997.

Floyd, Ronnie W. *The Power of Prayer and Fasting.* Nashville: Broadman and Holman Publishers, 1997.

Fortosis, Stephen. *A Treasury of Prayers.* Grand Rapids, MI: Kregel Publications, 2001.

Fuller, Cherri. *When Families Pray.* Sisters, OR: Multnomah Publishers, Inc., 1999.

_____. *When Children Pray.* Sisters, OR: Multnomah Publishers, Inc., 1998.

Gordon, S. D. *Quiet Talks on Prayer.* Uhrichsville, OH: Barbour Publishing, Inc., 1984. Out of print.

Hanegraaff, Hank. *The Prayer of Jesus.* Nashville: Word Publishing Group, 2001.

Heald, Cynthia. *Becoming a Woman of Prayer.* Colorado Springs: NavPress Publishing Group, 1996.

Hybels, Bill. *Too Busy Not to Pray*. Downers Grove, IL: InterVarsity Press, 1988.
Marshall, Catherine, *Adventures in Prayer*. Reissue ed. New York: Ballantine Books, 1990.
Mueller, George. *Answers to Prayer*. Chicago: Moody Press, 1984.
Nappa, Mike, and Amy Nappa. *52 Fun Family Prayer Adventures*. Minneapolis: Augsburg Books, 1996.
Murphey, Cecil. *Invading the Privacy of God*. Ann Arbor, MI: Servant Publications, 1997.
Omartian, Stormie. *The Power of a Praying Parent*. Eugene, OR: Harvest House Publishers, 1995.
_______. *The Power of a Praying Wife*. Eugene, OR: Harvest House Publishers, 1997.
_______. *Praying God's Will for Your Life*. Nashville: Thomas Nelson Publishers, 2001.
Spurgeon's Prayers. Great Britain: Christian Focus Publications, 1993.
Tirabassi, Becky. *Let Prayer Change Your Life*. Rev. ed. Nashville: Thomas Nelson Publishers, 2000.
Torrey, R. A. *How to Pray*. New Kensington, PA: Whitaker House, 1983.
Towns, Elmer. *Fasting for Spiritual Breakthrough*. Ventura, CA: Regal Books, 1996.

Bible Study

Arthur, Kay. *How to Study Your Bible*. Eugene, OR: Harvest House Publishers, 2001.
Hendricks, Howard G., and William D. Hendricks. *Living by the Book*. Chicago: Moody Press, 1991.
LaHaye, Tim. *How to Study the Bible for Yourself*. Rev. ed. Eugene, OR: Harvest House Publishers, 1998.
Lucado, Max. *Traveling Light: A Study of Psalm 23*. Nashville: Word Publishing Group, 2001.
Mears, Henrietta. *What the Bible Is All About*. Ventura, CA: Regal Books, 1998.
Miller, Kathy Collard. *An Expressive Heart: Stories, Lessons, and Exercises Inspired by the Psalms*. Lancaster, PA: Starburst Publishing, 2001.
Petersen, William, and Randy Petersen. *100 Bible Verses That Changed the World*. Grand Rapids, MI: Fleming H. Revell Company, 2000.
Richards, Larry. *The Bible—God's Word for the Biblically Inept*. Lancaster, PA: Starburst Publishing, 1998.
Sproul, R. C., and Robert Wolgemuth. *What's in the Bible*. Nashville: Word Publishing Group, 2001.
Yancey, Philip. *The Bible Jesus Read*. Grand Rapids, MI: Zondervan Publishing, 1999.

Worship

Donihue, Anita C. *When I'm Praising God*. Uhrichsville, OH: Barbour Publishing, Inc., 1999.
Hayford, Jack W. *Worship His Majesty*. Ventura, CA: Regal Books, 2000.
Kavanaugh, Patrick. *Worship: A Way of Life*. Grand Rapids, MI: Chosen Books, 2001.
Williamson, Alicia, and Sarah Groves. *A Seeking Heart: Rediscovering True Worship*. Birmingham, AL: New Hope Publishers, 2001.

Personal Witnessing

Burroughs, Esther. *Splash the Living Water.* Nashville: Thomas Nelson Publishers, 1999.

Fernando, Ajith, *Sharing the Truth in Love.* Grand Rapids, MI: Discovery House Publishers, 2001.

Lewis, C. S. *Mere Christianity.* San Francisco: HarperSanFrancisco, 2000.

Torrey, R. A. *How to Witness to Anyone.* New Kensington, PA: Whitaker House, 1986.

Solitude

Barnes, Emilie. *15 Minutes Alone with God.* Eugene, OR: Harvest House Publishers, 1994.

Rubietta, Jane. *Quiet Places.* Minneapolis: Bethany House Publishers, 1997.

_______. *Still Waters.* Minneapolis: Bethany House Publishers, 1999.

Journaling

Gire, Ken. *Reflections on Your Life: A Journal.* Colorado Springs: Chariot/Victor Publishing, 1998.

Hammarskjöld, Dag. *Markings.* New York: Ballantine Books, 1993.

Kelsey, Morton T. *Adventure Inward: Christian Growth Through Personal Journal Writing.* Minneapolis: Augsburg Fortress, 1980.

Peace, Richard. *Spiritual Journaling.* Colorado Springs: NavPress Publishing Group, 1999.

Personal Study

Glaspey, Terry W., ed. *A Passion for Books.* Eugene, OR: Harvest House Publishers, 1998. Out of print.

Miller, Calvin. *The Unchained Soul.* Minneapolis: Bethany House Publishers, 1999.

Petersen, William, and Randy Petersen, *100 Christian Books That Changed the Century.* Grand Rapids, MI: Fleming H. Revell Company, 2000.

Various Editors. *90 Days with the Christian Classics.* Nashville: Broadman and Holman Publishers, 1999.

Yancey, Philip, ed. *Reality and the Vision: 18 Contemporary Writers Tell Who They Read and Why.* Nashville: Word Publishing Group, 1990. Out of print.

Guidance

Blackaby, Henry T. *Experiencing God.* Nashville: Broadman and Holman Publishers, 1998.

Elliot, Elisabeth. *God's Guidance.* 2d. ed. Grand Rapids, MI: Fleming H. Revell Company, 1997.

Jeffress, Robert. *Hearing the Master's Voice.* Colorado Springs: WaterBrook Press, 2001.

Kise, Jane, and David Stark. *Life Directions.* Minneapolis: Bethany House Publishers, 1999.

LaHaye, Tim. *Finding the Will of God in a Crazy, Mixed-Up World.* Grand Rapids, MI: Zondervan Publishing House, 2001.

Packer, J. I. *God's Plan for You.* Wheaton, IL: Crossway Books, 2001.
Smith, Hannah Whitall. *The Christian's Secret of a Happy Life.* Reissue ed. New York: Ballantine Books, 1989.
ten Boom, Corrie. *This Day Is the Lord's.* Grand Rapids, MI: Baker Book House, 1999.
Torrey, R. A. *How to Succeed in the Christian Life.* New Kensington, PA: Whitaker House, 1984.

Simplicity

Barnes, Emilie. *Simply Organized.* Eugene, OR: Harvest House Publishers, 1997.
Bickel, Bruce, and Stan Jantz, *God Is in the Small Stuff and It All Matters.* Uhrichsville, OH: Promise Press, 1998.
Gordon, Arthur. *Return to Wonder.* Nashville: Broadman and Holman Publishers, 1996.
Jordan, Rebecca Barlow. *At Home in My Heart.* Uhrichsville, OH: Promise Press, 2001.
Lindbergh, Anne Morrow. *A Gift from the Sea.* New York: Pantheon Books, 1955.
Miller, Kathy Collard. *God's Abundance.* Lancaster, PA: Starburst Publishing, 1997.
Thomas, Kim. *Simplicity.* Nashville: Broadman and Holman Publishers, 1999.
Wright, H. Norman. *Simplify Your Life and Get More Out of It.* Forest, VA: American Association of Christian Counselors, 1998. Out of print.

Stewardship

Burkett, Larry. *Money Matters.* Nashville: Thomas Nelson Publishers, 2001.
Dacyczyn, Amy. *The Complete Tightwad Gazette.* New York: Random House, Inc., 1999.
Hunt, Mary. *The Complete Cheapskate.* Nashville: Broadman and Holman Publishers, 1998.
McGinn, Linda R., and T. R. Hollingsworth. *Investing Your Life in Things That Matter.* Nashville: Broadman and Holman Publishers, 1996.
Peel, Kathy. *The Family Manager.* Nashville: Word Publishing Group, 1996.

Service

Joiner, Barbara. *Yours for the Giving: Spiritual Gifts.* Rev. ed. Birmingham, AL: New Hope Publishers, 1999.
Stanley, Charles. *Developing a Servant's Heart.* Nashville: Thomas Nelson Publishers, 1998.
Swindoll, Charles. *Improving Your Serve.* Nashville: Word Publishing Group, 1981.
Wiersbe, Warren. *On Being a Servant of God.* Grand Rapids, MI: Baker Book House, 1999.

Sacrifice

Companjen, Anneke. *Hidden Sorrow, Lasting Joy.* Wheaton, IL: Tyndale House Publishers, 2001.
dc Talk and Voice of the Martyrs. *Jesus Freaks.* Tulsa, OK: Albury Publishing, 1999.
Hefley, Marti, and James Hefley. *By Their Blood: Christian Martyrs of the Twentieth Century.* Grand Rapids, MI: Baker Book House, 1996.

Index